The Lady from the Sea

Simon Stone

After Henrik Ibsen

I0141033

methuen | drama

LONDON • NEW YORK • OXFORD • NEW DELHI • SYDNEY

METHUEN DRAMA

Bloomsbury Publishing Plc, 50 Bedford Square, London, WC1B 3DP, UK
Bloomsbury Publishing Inc, 1359 Broadway, New York, NY 10018, USA
Bloomsbury Publishing Ireland, 29 Earlsfort Terrace, Dublin 2,
D02 AY28, Ireland

BLOOMSBURY, METHUEN DRAMA and the Methuen
Drama logo are trademarks of Bloomsbury Publishing Plc.

First published by Methuen Drama 2025

Design by Muse Creative Communications

Photography by Jason Bell

A catalogue record for this book is available from the British Library.

Library of Congress Control Number: 2025946228

ISBN: PB: 978-1-3506-0530-5
ePDF: 978-1-3506-0532-9
eBook: 978-1-3506-0531-2

Series: Modern Plays

Typeset by Mark Heslington Ltd, Scarborough, North Yorkshire

For product safety related questions contact
productsafety@bloomsbury.com.

To find out more about our authors and books visit
www.bloomsbury.com and sign up for our newsletters.

London Theatre Company in collaboration with Wouter van Ransbeek presents *The Lady from the Sea*

Ellida	Alicia Vikander
Edward	Andrew Lincoln
Hilda	Isobel Akuwudike
Heath	Joe Alwyn
Finn Marcet	Brendan Cowell
Lyle	John Macmillan
Asa	Gracie Oddie-James
Understudy Lyle/Heath	Daniel Gregory
Understudy Ellida	Sarah Moss
Understudy Hilda/Asa	Sadhbha Odufuwa-Bolger
Understudy Edward/Finn Marcet	Nathan Wiley

Writer & Director	Simon Stone
After	Henrik Ibsen
Set Designer	Lizzie Clachan
Costume Designer	Mel Page
Composition & Sound Design	Stefan Gregory
Lighting Designer	Nick Schlieper
Casting Director	Jessica Ronane CDG
Producer	Wouter van Ransbeek
Associate Director	Seán Linnen
Associate Lighting Designer	Guy Jones
Assistant Designer	Pip Terry
Intimacy Coordinator	David Thackeray
Costume Supervisor	Anna Josephs
Props Supervisor	Lily Mollgaard

The Lady from the Sea

Part One

One

Heath   Lovely day.

Edward   Isn't it?

Heath   You can see why they write poems about it.

Edward   Yeah.

Heath   The poets.

Edward   Yeah I know.

Heath   I've forgotten which ones.

Edward   Me too, I think.

Heath   An English country garden.

Edward   Listen, Heath –

Heath   Bad news?

Edward   No, no.

Heath   Not like me to forget a poet.

Edward   We need to wait for the blood tests.

Heath   Not a good omen. Forgetting a poet.

Edward   And then we can –

Heath   Are those roses or ranunculi? Not much of a flower man. Always wanted to be. Apparently there's an app.

Edward   Is there?

Heath   Identifies the species. So no diagnosis then?

Edward   The blood test will –

Heath   It's the prognosis I'm most worried about. It's likely something bothersome. That's an old-fashioned word. Where did that come from? The blood test will –

Edward   It could just as well be nothing.

Heath   Give me my gnoses. You suspect it's not though?

Edward   That's funny. Gnoses.

Heath   Not nothing.

Edward   It's my professional habit to –

Heath   But we're family though, aren't we?

Edward   Family, yeah.

Heath   Distant but nevertheless. You can't lie to family.

Edward   I think we lie to family more than anyone else. I don't care about hurting a stranger's feelings.

Heath   I envy you. There's a certain kind of freedom in that. Kipling.

Edward   I'll be perfectly honest with you as soon as I can.

Heath   'The Glory of the Garden'. So you don't consider me family? Not really?

Edward   Ah yes, Kipling.

Heath   Not enough to lie to me.

Edward   We'll get the results early next week. Try not to think about it too much.

Heath   'Come into the garden, Maud'.

Edward   Tennyson.

Heath   'Come Slowly – Eden!'

Edward   Emily Dickinson.

Heath   You're very good at this.

Edward   Lucky guess.

Heath   Aren't we two very well-educated Anglo-Saxon men?

Edward   I think it's about time for me to clock off.

Heath   A lot of coming in the garden.

Edward   Not in this garden.

Heath   That's a shame. Or maybe not.

Edward   I have two teenage daughters wandering around.

Heath   Not to forget 'The Garden of Love'.

Edward   Is that . . .?

Heath   Blake.

Edward   Wouldn't have got that one. All I know is 'Jerusalem'.

Heath   'Dark satanic mills' and all that.

Edward   'Bring me my bow . . .'

Heath   Mind you, he was right. Industrialisation has fucked us right and proper.

Edward   Although I do know my poets thanks to Instagram.

Heath   Instagram. I thought that was university?

Edward   God no. I was too busy drinking. I follow @poetsofinstagram or someone like that. There's another guy who sings Ancient Greek poetry in dialect. Beautiful voice. I'm much smarter than I was at university.

Heath   Is it useful knowledge though?

Edward   You'd have better luck with your ranunculi. With that app.

Heath   That's true. So I'll just have to wait 'til next week for my gnoses.

Edward   'Fraid so.

Heath   Rather unique isn't it, the 'gn' in English. Gnosis. Gnat.

Edward   Gnarly.

Heath   Gnashing. Which comes from gnathic as in Gnathostomata of course.

Edward   Of course.

Heath   We are insufferable.

Edward   Gnocchi.

Heath   Loanwords don't count.

Edward   Gnome.

Heath   Bringing us full circle back to the garden. Bravo. You see that? The glass is shaking in my hands.

Edward   Could just be nerves.

Asa   Dad, we're out of wine.

Edward   Hello to you too.

Asa   Hello. Hello. We're out of wine.

Edward   This is Heath. He's a cousin of yours.

Asa   I've never met you.

Heath   Several times removed. The Cornwall branch.

Asa   We have cousins in Cornwall? Weird.

Edward   How are we out of wine?

Asa   I drank it.

Edward   On your own?

Asa   Sure.

Edward   I bought a dozen bottles last week.

Asa   Oops.

Edward   Did Hilda have friends over again?

Asa   I plead the fifth.

Edward   I think your understanding of American jurisprudence needs a little work.

Asa   I think your face needs a little work.

Edward   She's usually a very polite young woman.

Asa   I'm working on getting out of my shell.

Heath   I think I might have overstayed my –

Asa   Dad has a parallel career as a life coach. 'Sit-ups might help with that belly.' 'You've got to work on your confidence around strangers.'

Edward   Which you're doing by publicly abusing your father.

Asa   Has he shown you his six-pack yet?

Edward   Why would I show my six-pack to a patient?

Asa   Just casually confirming its existence. Just by the by.

Edward   Asa.

Asa   Edward.

Edward   There's not even any rosé left?

Asa   There's some pét nat but I don't really know what that is.

Heath   Pétillant naturel.

Asa   Ah. Heath. You're one of those.

Heath   I am, I'm afraid.

Asa   Is that Japanese denim?

Heath   It is.

Asa   And you only wear second-hand leather. Which is why those boots are so hobo chic.

Edward   Stop it.

Asa   Lisbon or Athens?

Heath   Athens in autumn. Lisbon in Spring. Helsinki in summer.

Asa   Ferry to Tallinn.

Heath   Very cool for boutique shopping.

Edward   Are you flirting with my daughter?

Asa   Winter in Austria?

Heath   That's so early 2000s. You ever done Bulgaria?

Asa   Tell me more.

Edward   We don't do ski trips at all. I can drink pét nat.

Asa   Mum hated weird wines. Are you sick?

Heath   I don't know.

Edward   What have I said about –

Asa   What are your symptoms?

Edward   Asa.

Heath   I couldn't remember Rudyard Kipling's name just before.

Asa   Jesus I think we need to amputate.

Heath   She's funny.

Edward   I'll go to the wine shop.

Asa   No I can go. Give me the car keys.

Edward   I just got the car repaired, I'm not letting you –

Asa   Don't you have a patient?

Heath   I should get going.

Asa   Stay for dinner. We're having a little celebration.

Edward   No, Asa, Heath was just –

Heath   Yeah absolutely, get back to the hotel.

Asa   Have you got plans for dinner?

Heath   I was going to go for a walk along the lake.

Asa   Boring.

Edward   Asa.

Asa   Heath's our cousin.

Heath   If it's not too much of a bother . . .

Asa   It's not too much of a bother, is it, Dad?

Edward   No. It's. The more the merrier.

Asa   Brilliant. Now go get that wine.

Edward   Jesus Christ.

Asa   Any special requests, Heath? You're probably a craft beer type, aren't you?

Heath   I am.

Asa   Do you mix your own Bircher muesli?

Edward   Oh my God.

Asa   You do, don't you?

Edward   Don't let her bully you. I'll be back in ten.

Hilda   You going out? We don't have any wine left. I just saw.

Edward   Good evening, Dad, how was your day?

Hilda   He's started talking to himself.

Edward   How many friends did you have over last night?

Hilda   One or two.

Edward   How late were you up?

Asa   One or two.

Hilda   Not that late.

Edward   Did you make it to school on time?

Hilda   Yep.

Edward   I'm not going to get a call from them?

Hilda   No.

Asa   She's hoping the form tutor forgets.

Hilda   Didn't you say you were going to chuck Asa out when she finished high school?

Edward   Hilda.

Hilda   What do you even do around here?

Asa   I do your dirty washing for starters. You should see her –

Hilda   DON'T YOU EVEN –

Edward   HELLO. Hello, everyone. I'm Edward. I'm your father. I love you both. I want us all to get along.

Asa   We love you too.

Hilda   I feel ambivalent to positive feelings about you.

Edward   I'm going. This is Heath.

Exits.

Hilda   Are you sick?

Asa   He's our cousin.

Hilda   I've never met you.

Asa   Cornwall.

Hilda   That's weird. Everything on Dad's side is weird.

Heath   I haven't got my gnoses yet. Sorry just realising that joke needs context. This is nice here. Weather always this lovely?

Hilda   This is a scintillating conversation.

Edward   Sorry I just forgot. Have you seen Ellida?

Asa   I think she's down by the lake.

Hilda   Isn't she always down by the lake?

Asa   Hilda.

Hilda   What?

Edward   She left her phone on the bedside table.

Hilda   Like I say. Weird.

Asa   It's a beautiful day. Who needs their phone?

Edward   Says Madame TikTok. Alright I'll be back in ten.

Hilda   Oh, Dad. Lyle called. He's running a bit late.

Edward   When was he due?

Hilda   I dunno. 'Tell your dad I'm running a bit late.'

Edward   I'll call him.

Exits.

Hilda   Don't crash the car like certain members of this family like to do.

Asa   One of them was barely a scratch.

Heath   What's the celebration?

Hilda   Mum's birthday. I am so hungover.

Heath   I was under the impression that your generation didn't like drinking very much.

Hilda   I'm an anomaly.

Asa   Don't get drunk tonight.

Hilda   Tonight? Are you kidding?

Asa   I'm just saying.

Hilda   Seriously. You think I'd get drunk on Mum's birthday?

Asa   Maybe. I don't know.

Hilda   Fucking hell.

Asa   Sorry. What are you doing?

Heath   Trying to back off subtly.

Hilda   Major fail.

Heath   Is it odd having your father's medical practice at the bottom of your garden?

Hilda   Totally.

Asa   His medical practice pays for this house.

Hilda   Hey, Heath. Have you noticed anything particular about the nurses? We have a theory.

Heath   The nurses? No.

Hilda   Nothing about their appearance?

Heath   I feel like you're setting a trap.

Hilda   You don't find them particularly unattractive?

Heath   Well, that's . . .

Asa   Did you see the mole on Liliana's nose? Sometimes there's a single white hair growing out of it.

Heath   Wow, um . . .

Hilda   We think he's trying to prove he's not sleeping with them.

Asa   Unless of course he's into ugly chicks. An ingenious double fake.

Hilda   You didn't just say 'ugly chicks'.

Asa   I mean it requires an extraordinary effort to find two such exceptionally odd-looking women. Average-lookers are easy to find. Squint and turn your head sideways after a bottle of champagne and you accidentally end up in their pants-type women. But these two. They're specimens of clapped.

Heath   I for one don't set great store on surface aesthetics.

Hilda   Now that's a sentence.

Asa   Do you think it's just anthropological fascination? The ugly thing? Or is it a kink?

Heath   I think they're both very nice. And good at their jobs.

Hilda   You really don't care about the surface?

Heath   I can't say I do, no.

Hilda   What do you care about?

Heath   Empathy. Charm. Intelligence.

Hilda   Bullshit.

Asa   Total bullshit.

Hilda   You don't even notice what people look like?

Heath   In passing, maybe.

Hilda   And if someone's very beautiful, it has no impact on you? You've never had your breath taken away by how someone looks?

Heath   Can't say I remember such an occasion.

Hilda   That's sad.

Ellida   What are you guys talking about?

Asa   Nothing interesting.

Hilda   How was your swim?

Ellida   Sorry I didn't realise we had a guest.

Hilda   This is Heath. He's our cousin.

Heath   The lady of the house. My compliments on the beautiful . . . Actually. Wait. One second. One second. I know just the thing.

Exits.

Ellida   What was that?

Asa   He's a bit weird.

Hilda   I think he's asexual.

Ellida   And how did you find that out?

Hilda   We were talking about the –

Asa   Never mind. Hilda's just being provocative. We'll leave you alone. I'm sure you want some peace and quiet.

Ellida   No, I was actually . . .

Asa   Come on, Hilda.

Hilda   Ow. Don't pull me.

They exit. **Ellida** *is alone. She lays her towel out on the lawn. Lies on it. After a while,* **Lyle** *enters. He watches her in silence. She notices him eventually.*

Ellida   How long have you been standing there?

Lyle   Between fifteen and thirty seconds. You look amazing.

Ellida   Bringing up old memories?

Lyle   No comment. How's your husband?

Ellida   I don't know where he is.

Lyle   Getting booze. He called me. Your phone's on the bedside table.

Ellida   Is it? I must have forgotten it today.

Lyle   Liberated from technology. I'm impressed.

Ellida   Want a glass of wine?

Lyle   You drinking?

Ellida   Not at the moment.

Lyle   Tonight? Or . . .?

Ellida   Last few months. Not since . . .

Lyle   Right. Ed told me.

Ellida   Yep.

Lyle   Want a hug?

Ellida   Not from you.

Lyle   I won't drink if you're not.

Ellida   Edward's been drinking.

Lyle   Too much?

Ellida   I don't know. What do you think?

Lyle   I was in South Africa for half the year. Honestly we're due a catch-up.

Ellida   Please do that. He needs to talk to someone.

Lyle   Yes, ma'am.

Ellida   Don't call me that.

Lyle   Sorry, sir.

Ellida   Someone just called me the lady of the house.

Lyle   You are.

Ellida   That lake is depressing.

Lyle   It takes quite some determination to find Ullswater depressing.

Ellida   There's no salt. There's no waves. No sand between your toes.

Lyle   No. It's a lake. Lakes do swimming differently. The freshwater rural idyll type of swimming. Some people prefer lakes.

Ellida   I need the sea.

Lyle   Then book something.

Ellida   I can't. I need to get some work done. I'm way behind on my deadline.

Lyle   Well, if it's late already, another week won't hurt. What about my place in Formentera?

Ellida   Ugh.

Lyle   Wow. You're determined to be in a bad mood.

Ellida   I'm sorry. No. I'm not sorry.

Lyle   Beyonce.

Ellida   What?

Lyle   Really? Have you started the novel?

Ellida   Don't talk about the book. Where've you come from?

Lyle   Manchester. I'm living in Manchester.

Ellida   Is that fun?

Lyle   I just moved in with someone.

Ellida   A human being?

Lyle   A female human being.

Ellida   You're kidding me.

Lyle   My heart rate is elevated just talking about it.

Ellida In a good way?

Lyle I'm fucking terrified.

Ellida Then why?

Lyle Because I don't want to die alone in a nursing home.

Ellida You probably will anyway.

Lyle Thanks.

Ellida I'll come visit. Bring you vintage porn.

Lyle You know me so well.

Ellida How's that libido going? Undiminished as ever?

Lyle You'd be surprised. I can go for long pleasant walks without spying the closest place for a quickie.

Ellida Jesus. I remember.

Lyle Yeah.

Ellida The toilets at the Serpentine Gallery.

Lyle Oh right. Yeah.

Ellida What's her name?

Lyle I don't want to jinx it.

Ellida So you haven't asked her her name yet?

Lyle Jesus. Susannah. There you go. I've ruined it.

Ellida You like her.

Lyle I really like her.

Ellida Fuck me. Even Lyle's growing up.

Edward Is he? What happened?

Ellida Susannah happened.

Edward Ooh. Do tell.

Ellida   You are only sleeping with one woman right? Or I'll have to hit you.

Lyle   Just one.

Ellida   Since the beginning?

Lyle   Weeeell.

Ellida   You are so fucking annoying.

Lyle   Since we've been exclusive.

Ellida   And that was?

Lyle   A couple of. A week or two ago. A week ago. Five days min.

Ellida   Okay. I'm not investing. I've already forgotten her name.

Lyle   You're the one who made me say it.

Ellida   Invite me to the wedding. Until then, fuck off. He only has to have sex once a day now.

Lyle   I didn't say that.

Edward   I hate you.

Ellida   Me too. We, as a couple, hate you.

Lyle   Well, I envy the two of you.

Edward   No, mate. Don't do that.

Ellida   Hey. Why d'you say that?

Edward   Ow.

Ellida   I'm having a shower. Get that muddy water off me.

Edward   People kill to live near Ullswater, Ellida.

She's gone.

If only her grumpiness wasn't so attractive. Don't say anything.

Lyle   I wasn't going to. She doesn't seem as bad as you made out.

Edward   Well, good. Maybe she was just missing company. This is good. Thanks for coming. You look chiselled and manly.

Lyle   You too. Jogging?

Edward   Ten miles a day. Except Sundays.

Lyle   Nice jogs around here.

Edward   Screaming in the woods.

Lyle   Good on you.

Edward   It's okay. I'm okay. Just shit timing.

Lyle   I know.

Edward   And we haven't really spoken about it.

Lyle   Are you avoiding each other?

Edward   Kind of. I suggest dates every now and then so we can . . .

Lyle   And they don't happen?

Edward   Never really commits. And then on the day there's a migraine. Or a bad period or –

Lyle   She's having those? That's good.

Edward   Yeah.

Lyle   You reckon you'll try again? You haven't been speaking. You haven't discussed it yet.

Edward   Oh, man.

Lyle   What about you? Do you want to?

Edward   I've almost got Asa and Hilda out the house . . .

Lyle   Was it her idea? The first pregnancy?

Edward   Kind of. She certainly brought it up a lot.

Lyle   Who popped the condoms on the shelf?

Edward   She did. She said, let's see what happens. But we weren't keeping an eye on her cycle or anything.

Lyle   Just shagging like two hot people in love.

Edward   Don't.

Lyle   I was only imagining it a little bit.

Edward   It's been five very fucking weird years.

Lyle   Dude.

Edward   Everyone's got their tragedies.

Lyle   Aisha would be proud of you, man.

Edward   I don't know.

Lyle   I know she would. Asa and Hilda are –

Edward   Out of control.

Lyle   They're teenagers, man. They're young women. They're supposed to be out of control. I'd be worried if they weren't.

Edward   Hilda still texting you?

Lyle   Pretty much daily.

Edward   What do you guys even talk about?

Lyle   Sometimes about her mum. Mostly about Kendrick lyrics.

Edward   What do you say about Aisha?

Lyle   That she loved her.

Edward   Thank you.

Lyle   That it's a damn shame she's missed who Hilda's become.

Edward   Alright this is getting soppy.

Lyle   Sorry.

Edward   No it's good. It's good. Scream some more in the woods tomorrow.

Lyle   A 'barbaric yawp'!

Edward   Walt Whitman.

Lyle   No. Robin Williams. *Dead Poets Society*.

Edward   He was quoting Whitman you nincompoop.

Lyle   Bringing nincompoop back. I like it. Whitman, eh? Is he on Instagram?

Edward   I really do hate you.

Lyle   Let it out. Come on. I can handle it.

Edward   You in love?

Lyle   Maybe. Maybe.

Edward   Try not to fuck it up.

Lyle   Any tips?

Edward   I'm really the wrong person to ask.

Hilda   LYLE!

Lyle   HILDA!

Hilda   How long have you been here? Why didn't you text?

Lyle   I thought you might hear me.

Edward   You are very loud.

Lyle   I know. I know. Fuck, Ed. The other day a woman told me on the way out of a restaurant that I'd ruined her whole evening. Because of my loud laughing.

Hilda   That's so cruel.

Edward   You can laugh as loud as you like here.

Lyle   My foghorn.

Hilda   Your nuclear meltdown alarm.

Lyle   My laugh is the last sound you hear before the apocalypse.

Hilda   I missed you.

Lyle   Can I hug you? Ellida wouldn't let me.

Edward   You never asked me.

Lyle   Sorry, man, you want a hug?

Edward   I don't need your charity.

Hilda   Come on then. A short one.

Lyle   Okay. Incoming.

Hilda   Okay.

Edward   Isn't that sweet.

Lyle   See? Hugs are soothing. A soothing evening hug for Hilda.

Hilda   You're really ruining it.

Lyle   You know who's great at hugs? Dads. Dads love hugs.

Edward   Thanks, buddy. Glad I shared that with you.

Lyle   When's the last time you guys just hugged it out?

Hilda   This is irritating, Lyle.

Lyle   Then tell me to shut my mouth.

Hilda   Shut your mouth, Lyle.

Lyle   Fierce. Love it.

Ellida *has come out and now she wraps her arms around* **Edward** *from behind.*

Ellida   I missed you today.

Hilda   Would you like a glass of wine, Lyle?

Lyle   Everyone's trying to get me drunk.

Hilda   Back in a sec.

Edward   I bought rosé and cab sav. I should start the barbecue.

Ellida   See that? They run away whenever I appear.

Edward   Well, you did grope her father right in front of her.

Ellida   That was a grope? Really?

Edward   A minor grope.

Ellida   Lyle?

Lyle   Definitely PG rated. Not even near a grope.

Edward   He's always on your side. I don't know why the girls get nervous when you're around.

Ellida   So you admit it.

Lyle   You are banging their father. Now, I'm not a psychoanalyst . . .

Edward   The world breathes a sigh of relief.

Ellida   We were getting on really well. Like, really well. Until I got pregnant.

Lyle   Shit.

Ellida   I get it. I get it. I'd be angry. If I was a teenager and this bitch turned up and stole my father's attention.

Edward   That's not how they think of you. And you know how much I hate the word bitch.

Ellida   Especially after everything that happened.

Lyle   It's complicated. That's for sure.

Heath   Here. We. Are.

Edward   Oh my goodness.

Heath   Now you probably already know about the place with freshly cut flowers down the hill but there was a lovely hand-drawn sign next to a farm on the drive up here and then I heard it was your birthday and I thought screw it, I'll just drive back quickly and they'd actually already closed but I told them there was an important celebration underway and so, TA DA! Happy birthday to you, happy birthday to –

Edward   Um. Heath.

Heath   Nobody else joining in?

Ellida   I'm sorry.

Heath   I knew it. I went too big. Never even met you before and now I bought half the flower shop.

Ellida   No, it's not my birthday.

Heath   Oh. Did I . . .?

Edward   I can explain.

Heath   The girls said they were celebrating their mother's birthday. Were they just pulling my –

Ellida   No.

Edward   My wife's dead.

Heath   Oh.

Edward   My former wife. I mean we were married when she died. Now I'm married to Ellida.

Heath   I thought you looked very young to have two teenage daughters.

Ellida   I could have had children their age.

Edward   Could you?

Ellida   In another life. Sure.

Heath   I'm such a dolt.

Lyle Dolt. Wow. All these old-fashioned insults flying around today. I need to keep notes.

Heath My nan did tell me something about this before I came. I completely forgot it. I'm so sorry.

Ellida And I'm sorry I forgot Aisha's birthday. Were you scared of telling me?

Edward I'm the dolt.

Lyle You're the nincompoop.

Edward I kept meaning to tell you and I –

Ellida Strange. I remembered last year.

Edward You've had a lot on your mind.

Ellida You don't need to be careful around me. I'm actually quite tough. Maybe you don't know that.

Edward Sorry.

Lyle Everyone's sorry apart from me. I'm so not sorry. I turned up only ten minutes late. I brought chocolates and an assortment of strange spices, rubs and salt mixes from the farmers' market, I brought –

Edward Can you please stop doing that. We never use them. I mean never. If I want to use spices I make my own mixes. I have no interest in other people's mixes. They're a waste of money. It's token friendship. Find a gift I'll actually use. The chocolates we'll eat. The spices we'll throw away.

Ellida I'll try your spice mix.

Edward Washing-up liquid. That's something that's always running out. Buy me that. Buy me toilet paper. An oldie but a goodie. Tinned tuna never goes astray. Buy me a wooden spatula. They break and you're frustrated because they're essential cooking aids. Some pseudo-chef's cajun spice mix is not. Not essential. Not wanted. Not appreciated. And stop leaving the price tag on so I know how expensive it was.

Lyle   Well, now I'm sorry too.

Ellida   Ed. That was.

Edward   He needs to be told. It'll never stop otherwise. Will you stop now?

Lyle   Uh huh. Yeah.

Ellida   Will you stop now?

Edward   I'm already finished. I said what I needed to say. Now I need a glass of rosé.

Asa   Coming. How many glasses?

Ellida   I'll have one too.

Edward   Really?

Ellida   I told you. Stop worrying about me.

Edward   I knew inviting Lyle would be great for you.

Asa   So how many glasses?

Edward   Bring six. We'll all have a toast to Aisha.

Ellida   She made two beautiful young women.

Heath   I'm sorry about the flowers. Do you have enough vases? I have a bucket in my car if you need it.

Hilda   Why do you have a bucket in your car?

Edward   I'm going to get the briquettes lit.

Lyle   I missed you, shorty.

Hilda   Don't ruin my hairdo.

Lyle   You call that a hairdo? Girl, you've been in the country way too long.

Asa   Hey, weirdo. Dad bought you craft beer.

Heath   Ooh this one's good. I read on a blog about this one.

Asa   Of course you did. Come help me bring out the chairs.

Ellida   We used to have evenings like this on the beach when I was growing up.

Lyle   Hey, Ellie.

Ellida   Yeah?

Lyle   I've already dialled up 'Light Nostalgia' on my Spotify.

Ellida   Fuck you.

Lyle   No thanks. I'm newly monogamous.

Edward   Do we really have to do the vegan stuff separate from the rest, Hilda?

Hilda   Oh. My. God.

Edward   Just asking. I need a second barbecue, fuck.

Two

Edward   So what do you think?

Lyle   Well, I'd need to see the blood tests.

Edward   But it doesn't look good.

Lyle   No.

Edward   Poor bastard. He's only twenty-eight.

Lyle   Jesus.

Edward   What would you do? If you knew you only had a year or two left?

Lyle   Take an overdose.

Edward   I mean if it wasn't neurodegenerative.

Lyle   It's ALS man. That guy's going to struggle to string a sentence together in six months.

Edward   But if it wasn't.

Lyle   What, cancer?

Edward   Sure.

Lyle   But not brain. Because then we're back to me losing my cognitive functions.

Edward   Bowel. Or pancreas.

Lyle   Colostomy bag. That's going to affect my bucket list.

Edward   Lung?

Lyle   This is a fun game. Choose your favourite cancer with Ed and Lyle.

Edward   Would you stay with this girl you just met?

Lyle   Fuck. That's a good question.

Edward   Would she stay with you?

Lyle   You know what, I have a feeling Susannah's the kind of person who would.

Edward   Wow. Empty your colostomy bag for you.

Lyle   Hold me while I drool.

Edward   Now that's romance.

Lyle   Poor dude.

Hilda   Who? Heath?

Lyle   How'd you know I was talking about him?

Hilda   Is he dying?

Edward   We're all dying.

Hilda   But, like, is he dying soon?

Edward   I don't know.

Hilda   But you think so?

Edward   Have you heard of –

Hilda   Doctor–patient confidentiality bla bla just wink at me. Once for yes. Twice for no.

Edward   I'm not blinking for you.

Hilda   Sure you're not.

Edward   I'm really not.

Hilda   Hang on that was three, what does that mean?

Edward   Hilda, I am not blinking for you. My eyes are dry.

Hilda   Lyle?

Lyle   Don't do that. Don't use my love against me.

Hilda   Aw, you love me? Did you just blink once? He's dying?

Lyle   Neither of us are transmitting messages with our eyelids.

Hilda   I really hope he's dying.

Edward   HILDA.

Hilda   I know. It's terrible. But you told me I should tell you the truth. No matter how dark my thoughts.

Edward   Sorry.

Hilda   Do you think he'd stay in touch with me if I asked?

Lyle   What do you mean?

Hilda   Like would he send me videos from his hospital bed? Oh my God do you think he'd let me visit him in hospital?

Lyle   Watching someone die is not fun.

Hilda   Sometimes seeing the worst thing imaginable is fascinating. *Terrifier 3* isn't fun per se. It's horrifying. But there's something moreish about it.

Lyle   Holy shit she's seen *Terrifier 3*.

Edward   What the hell is *Terrifier 3*?

Lyle   Guy gets a chainsaw up his ass.

Edward   Jesus Christ, Hilda.

Hilda   This is a judgement-free zone, Edward.

Edward   Who showed you that movie? Was it Jessica? I bet it was Jessica.

Hilda   Dad.

Edward   Bloody Jessica.

Hilda   DAD.

Edward   I don't like her. She always smiles at me as if butter wouldn't melt in her bloody *Terrifier 3* a chainsaw up his what?

Lyle   His ass.

Edward   How the hell did they film that?

Hilda   That's what I wondered. Can you set up the next appointment with Heath when I'm home from school? Make it a late afternoon appointment. Then I can be casually doing my homework in the garden and –

Edward   Well, that will be suspicious from the get-go. You doing homework.

Hilda   He'll be crying or having a panic attack and I'll ask him what's wrong and he'll tell me about the diagnosis and maybe he'll need a hug and –

Lyle   You're a sociopath.

Edward   If. That were to happen. If. I would send him to a counsellor. And that person would be the best qualified to –

Hilda   But counsellors can't wipe the tears off your face or give you an empathetic kiss or –

Edward   Do you fancy him?

Hilda   He's a total dork. But throw the inevitable existential despair into the mix and –

Lyle   You're a sociopath.

Hilda   Nothing ever *happens* here. It's all spring flowers and pleasant walks by the lake and fucking chai lattes and focaccia. Sundried fucking tomatoes. Gossip about who went to what base with whom at Freddie's house on the weekend. Smoking weed in the Argos car park. Who's got the best bikini dance on TikTok. Missing cats and the farmer who got drunk and slammed his tractor into the heritage-listed clock tower.

Edward   If you're looking for someone to look after, people die in the country too.

Hilda   But not hot young dorks that had so much still ahead of them. Not the tragedy of a life cut off too short. Sorry.

Edward   Yep.

Hilda   Yeah. Okay. Sorry.

Lyle   Maybe that's why you're fascinated by him. Because of your mum.

Hilda   Well, he's not going to kill himself like Mum.

Edward   Okay. Um. I'm genuinely trying not to judge but . . .

Hilda   What? Did I say something wrong? Am I not supposed to mention it?

Asa   Hey. Hilda.

Hilda   That's what happened isn't it?

Asa   Slow down.

Ellida   What's going on?

Hilda   I'm not supposed to talk about suicide, apparently.

Heath   Suicide? Why are we talking about suicide?

Lyle   Guys.

Ellida   It's okay, Hilda.

Hilda   How do you know?

Ellida   I don't.

Hilda   No. You don't. So stay out of it.

Edward   Don't talk to her like that.

Hilda   You know what? Fuck you. And you. Fuck all of you.

Asa   Hilda . . .

Edward   You? Or me?

Asa   I'll go. I'm taking this bottle.

Edward   Don't.

She does.

I'm sorry about that.

Ellida   Don't be sorry.

Edward   No but it's not fair.

Ellida   You should have seen me as a teenager.

Lyle   Unlucky combination of hormones and grief.

Edward   I don't try to avoid talking about it.

Ellida   No you don't.

Edward   I'm happy to talk about it.

Lyle   Sure.

Edward   Not happy. I don't mean that. You know what I mean.

Ellida   We do.

Lyle   None of this stuff is easy to negotiate. I think you're doing a good job of it.

Edward   Thanks, Lyle. I think so too. I mean am I fucking them up? Is that what I'm doing?

Heath quotes the first line of Philip Larkin's 'This Be the Verse', 'They fuck you up your mum and dad. They may not mean to, but they do.'

Edward   Larkin. Thank you, Heath.

Lyle   Who is this guy? A walking Wikipedia? You're annoying, man.

Heath   I get that a lot.

Lyle   'Cause you're annoying. People like me don't like people like you.

Heath   Smart people?

Lyle   You're not the only smart person here.

Heath   Glad to hear it.

Lyle   I operate on brains. I know a lot about brains.

Heath   Right.

Lyle   I know all about the squishy grey bit where you keep all that meaningless knowledge.

Heath   Got it.

Lyle   And for all the other bullshit, I've got ChatGPT. So people like you are just window dressing.

Heath   Aha.

The radio, which has been playing through an outdoor speaker, has cut to the news. **Ellida** *has started listening closely.*

Edward   What is it?

Ellida *goes to the speaker and turns it up.*

News   . . . who was found responsible for the death of Olly Johnson, a British security guard and father of two children. The crime occurred at BP's newly opened oil rig off the coast of Norway in 2006. The release of Finn Marcet has brought tensions to the surface in the quiet Yorkshire town Johnson hails from. His nineteen-year-old daughter had this to say: 'I never met my father because of that man, so I can't see why he should be treated like –'

Ellida *has switched the radio off.*

Silence.

Edward   Ellida? Are you okay?

Heath   Fascinating case, Finn Marcet. Kind of a proto Luigi Mangione. The radical left went absolutely crazy for him. I mean the guy mercilessly threw a man off of a North Sea oil rig but –

Ellida   Were you there?

Heath   In the middle of the North Sea at the age of six? No. No I wasn't.

Ellida   You have no idea what happened.

Heath   I mean reputable news outlets have been fairly unequivocal. I didn't realise –

Ellida   The journalists weren't there either. There was a wild storm that night and . . .

Silence. They're looking at her. She laughs.

Edward   How do you know all that, Ellida?

Ellida   Well, he's talking about the radical left, and I actually –

Edward   I don't think he meant any offence in the term.

Heath   You used to be –

Ellida   I used to dabble.

Lyle   That's news to me.

Edward   Me too . . .

Ellida   You don't know everything about my past.

Edward   Okay.

Ellida   I haven't told you everything.

Edward   Okay.

Ellida   I thought that was our deal.

Edward   I guess it was.

Ellida   Neither of us would delve too –

Edward   What, were you an activist?

Ellida   Um . . .

Heath   I'm sorry. I really didn't mean any offence. Maybe radical left wasn't the right, I mean maybe it has pejorative connotations but I wasn't really, just trying to make conversation really, I tend to get verbal when I feel awkward and yeah it's happening now, I'm talking and you're watching me and I know everyone wishes I'd stop but somehow –

Lyle   Maybe we should –

Heath   Yep. Thank you. Didn't know how to stop.

Lyle   Shall we walk back to the hotel?

Heath   Love it.

Edward   You are staying here tonight, Lyle?

Lyle   I booked the hotel. Should I have –

Edward   You always stay here?

Lyle   I've been up at all hours recently. Didn't want to bother anyone with my –

Edward   Oh. Okay.

Lyle   Sorry. I should have discussed it with you.

Edward   Will we see you in the morning? For breakfast?

Lyle   Sure if you want? Ellida?

Ellida   Yeah. Come by.

Lyle   Okay . . . Come on, window dressing.

Heath   Thank you so much for a lovely. Yeah.

Edward   Yeah.

Heath   And I'll. Next week.

Edward   Sure.

Heath   I'm sorry.

Ellida   No it's. Fine.

Heath *and* **Lyle** *exit.*

Edward   Do you want a glass of wine?

Ellida   I don't know.

Edward   What's going on?

Ellida   I don't know I . . . Is it really hot here all of a sudden?

Edward   No.

Ellida *gives him a long look. Shakes her head.*

Edward   You don't have to tell me anything.

Ellida   I don't know why I never brought it up. I mean maybe I do. Fuck. Ed.

Edward   Hey. Slow down.

Ellida   You don't understand. This was. This was a big part of my life.

Edward   What was?

Ellida   He was.

Edward   Who's he?

Ellida Um . . .

Edward Listen. You don't have to tell me about it.

Ellida Maybe I shouldn't.

Edward But it seems to be gnawing at you.

Ellida I haven't thought about any of this for years. For years, Ed, and now all of a sudden . . .

Edward Was this the news? Just now on the radio?

Ellida You said I don't have to tell you about it.

Edward Sorry.

Ellida Oh fuck. Can you just hold me?

He does. She gets up almost straight away.

Just ask me.

Edward Okay.

Ellida Go.

Edward Did you know the man who died?

Ellida Wrong question.

Edward Okay. You said him.

Ellida Yeah but not him. Not him. I didn't know him. I'd never met him before.

Edward Okay. The killer?

Ellida Finn isn't a murderer.

Edward Finn. You remember his name.

Ellida Of course I remember his name.

Edward Right.

Ellida Keep asking. Otherwise I'll –

Edward You knew him?

Ellida   Yes.

Edward   You knew him well?

Ellida   Yes.

Edward   Were you and him –

Ellida   Yes.

Edward   For how long?

Ellida   A year. A year and a half. Um . . .

Edward   It's okay.

Ellida   Okay stop asking.

Edward   You loved him.

Ellida   I said STOP.

Edward   It's okay.

Ellida   Stop telling me it's okay. It's not okay. Okay? It's not okay. None of this is okay.

Asa   Dad? Did something happen? Where did everyone go?

Edward   Asa, go away.

Asa   Excuse me?

Edward   Go away. Now.

Asa   What the fuck? This is my house.

Ellida   She doesn't need to go anywhere.

Edward   Ellida.

Ellida   I want her to stay. Asa, come here. Sit down with us.

Edward   Ellida, please.

Ellida   How's your honours going? We're always so preoccupied we never ask.

Asa   I delivered last month. I have my thesis defence next week.

Ellida   Wow. You must be nervous.

Asa   I don't. I feel like it's quite a niche subject and the professors are kind of over-impressed with me so I'm hoping they don't go too easy on me.

Ellida   Maybe the external evaluator will bring a little spice to the proceedings.

Edward   I actually can't believe.

Ellida   Ed. We can continue this later. Or tomorrow. Please.

Asa   Are you guys having a fight?

Edward   Yes.   **Ellida**   No.

Asa   Well, that's clarified that.

Ellida   Hey. Ed. Give me a kiss.

Asa   Please don't do that in front of me.

Ellida *gives* **Edward** *a long kiss.*

Asa   And she did.

Three

Lyle   And I accidentally said, 'Love you, bye.' Just like that. I love you, bye. Like I was talking to my mum.

Asa   *Très* Freudian.

Lyle   I *know*. Do you think she noticed that?

Asa   She definitely noticed it. Aw that's kind of cute. You projected motherliness onto her. Would she be a good mother?

Lyle   She'd be an amazing mother. Without a doubt.

Asa   Aw cute. You're thinking of reproducing.

Lyle   Stop saying aw cute to everything I say.

Asa   You're opening up your soul to another human being. That is truly unprecedented.

Lyle   It's not at all unprecedented.

Asa   It's unprecedented for an emotional delinquent like you.

Lyle   I don't want her to mother me.

Asa   Think deep and hard about what you just said. And whether it's true. Take your time.

Lyle   Fuck off. Okay I do like it when I'm sick and she goes out to Boots to get me medicine and makes a chicken and vegetable soup from scratch.

Asa   And gives you a sneaky blowjob in a nurse outfit.

Lyle   You are my best friend's daughter, you cannot be talking to me like that.

Asa   I'm not coming onto you.

Lyle   I'm aware of that. But still. Asa.

Asa   Yeah.

Lyle   I'm going to ask an annoyingly paternal question.

Asa   Oh fuck.

Lyle   Are you still doing that OnlyFans account?

Asa   No.

He raises his eyebrows.

Yeah I am still doing it. Living overseas isn't cheap, man.

Lyle   Overseas?

Asa   I got an offer for a PhD at Yale. They read my thesis.

Lyle   Wow.

Asa   One of my supervisors sent it to them.

Lyle   Wow.

Asa   I know. Fucking Yale.

Lyle   Isn't it like a hundred grand a year to study at Yale?

Asa   They've offered me a scholarship.

Lyle   Holy shit.

Asa   But I still have to pay for accom and living expenses.

Lyle   You could wait tables at the hotel.

Asa   Do you know how much more money I make in much less time online?

Lyle   You don't do full –

Asa   No, Lyle. It's just teasy stuff. Like when I'm having a shower or –

Lyle   I really don't want to know.

Asa   Have you been to the page?

Lyle   Just the account page. I was making sure you –

Asa   So you did know I was still doing it?

Lyle   I knew the page was still there, I didn't know if you were actively –

Asa   You were checking whether I'd lie to you.

Lyle   Yes.

Asa   Why?

Lyle   Okay. Um. Your mother sent me an email before she –

Asa   Topped herself.

Lyle   Don't be like Hilda.

Asa   She's right. Edward pretends it didn't happen. The way he talks about it, it's like she slipped away unexpectedly in her sleep. A forty-year-old woman. In her prime. That's not what. She made a decision. She drove to the quarry and fucking . . .

Pause.

She sent you an email?

Lyle   That night.

Asa   She didn't send us an email.

Lyle   I'm sorry.

Asa   Would have appreciated an email.

Lyle   I hadn't brought it up because –

Asa   Yeah you hadn't. Does Dad know?

Lyle   I should have told him first but then –

Asa   You needed to talk me out of doing homemade porn.

Lyle   Right and –

Asa   It's not porn.

Lyle   It's not?

Asa   No. It's seriously softcore. Other people I know are inviting two dudes over and –

Lyle   Jesus. Don't do that.

Asa   Why not?

Lyle   Asa.

Asa   It's no skin off my nose. I'm not even into dudes.

Lyle   You're not?

Asa   All these revelations. Poor shocked Lyle. Needs his lovermother even more now.

Lyle   Please don't call Susannah my lovermother.

Asa   Motherlover is better, you're right.

Lyle   Why not go straight to motherfucker.

Asa   No, that's you. You're the motherfucker. She's the motherfuckee.

Lyle   I really need a second go at saying I love her the first time.

Asa   You don't get a second go at the first time. You fucked it. You Lyled it.

Lyle   I totally Lyled it.

Asa   Make the second time you say it really hot and unexpected.

Lyle   Challenge accepted.

Asa   Why do you like Hilda more than me?

Lyle   I don't.

Asa   You text her all the time. She's always laughing at her phone and whenever I ask, she says oh it's Lyle and walks away secretively.

Lyle   She's trying to make you jealous and you fell for it.

Asa   Cow.

Lyle   I text you too and you never answer.

Asa   I'm busy. I'm going to Yale, bitch.

Lyle   And I respect that. But Hilda needs someone to offload to.

Asa   I should be that. Her sister. Not creepy Lyle.

Lyle   You think I'm creepy?

Asa   No but. If she told a social worker she was texting a man twenty years older than her . . .

Lyle   Twenty-five. That's a quarter of a century.

Asa   Hang on. How old are you? I thought you were in your thirties?

Lyle   Mid-forties.

Asa   What the fuck?

Lyle   Beige don't age. You have those benefits to look forward to, baby.

Asa   So what? This email. She told you to look after us, or what?

Lyle   Um. Yeah.

Asa   And what? Make sure they don't end up smoking crack and selling their bodies?

Lyle   Other words but –

Asa   That's not what I'm doing.

Lyle   Okay.

Asa   I mean if you did watch my OnlyFans, which you shouldn't.

Lyle   Which I definitely will not.

Asa   What you'd see is. I'm doing things I would have done anyway. It's just my normal life. Taking a shower. Getting dressed. Getting undressed and going to bed. Having a wank every now and then. And if some horny old dude wants to pay my way through Yale University and set me on my way to taking over the world then –

Lyle   But some of this stuff leaks and then –

Asa   So what? People know what I look like naked? I don't care.

Lyle   A future partner of yours might.

Asa   Then they're not the right partner for me.

Lyle   Listen, Asa –

Asa   I know this must be breaking your brain.

Lyle   If this ever becomes traumatic for you.

Asa   Why would it? I just described to you what I –

Lyle   But if for whatever reason you're surprised and all of a sudden it feels weird or brings up –

Asa   What would it bring up?

Lyle   Just promise me. You'll let me know. And I'll help you find someone less creepy and male and ancient to talk to.

Asa   I won't need it.

Lyle   Asa.

Asa   I promise. What are you doing?

Lyle   Say it again. I'll record it.

Asa   I promise, Lyle. Thank you, Lyle. You're my hero, Lyle.

Lyle   I'm sending you that every six months.

Asa   You are such a headache. Thanks, Mum. You lumbered me with a fifty-year-old baby as a guardian.

Lyle   I said mid-forties, don't exaggerate please. You don't like men?

Asa   Oh. GOD.

Four

Ellida   What a beautiful walk. What a beautiful swim.

Heath   It was gorgeous. Thanks for inviting me.

Edward   Always happy to have a virtual stranger join my early morning outings with my wife.

Ellida   Look at that tree, it's started blooming since last night. Look at that, darling.

Edward   That's the apple tree.

Heath   Oh so it is. I downloaded that app by the way. Super-useful.

Ellida   Hang on. That's an apple tree? Mind blown.

Edward   You know it's the apple tree.

Ellida   I've never seen apples on that tree.

Edward   Yes you have.

Ellida   No I haven't. I would have noticed that. I would have noticed apples.

Edward   It's a very productive tree.

Ellida   It hasn't been producing while I've been here. Maybe I jinxed it. Maybe I rendered it fruitless. Do you know what the word for fertile is in Swedish?

Edward   Tell me.

Ellida   *Fruktbar.* Fruitful.

Heath   This is a very fruitful conversation.

Ellida   And the word for infertile?

Edward   This is fun.

Ellida   *Ofruktbar.* Unfruitful. That tree is infertile.

Edward   Are we trying to have an intimate conversation in front of Heath?

Ellida   You poor thing. Your tree and your wife are not currently bearing fruit.

Edward   Maybe both of them need a break. And I don't necessarily need fruit. I can do without fruit.

Ellida   Can you?

Edward   I am not the tree.

Ellida *laughs.*

Edward   What?

Ellida   We truly bludgeoned that metaphor to death.

Edward   I'm sorry. Not much of a poet.

Ellida   I wrote five pages today. I'm on fire.

Edward   I was wondering what you were doing up at five.

Ellida   Oh that's right. You've never known that. I have to start writing before the sun rises.

Edward   There's so much I don't know apparently.

Heath   I'm so fascinated by different people's creative processes. I have to sculpt naked for example.

Edward   And delete.

Ellida   You're a sculptor? Did I know that?

Heath   Well, I sculpt. Or mostly plan sculptures. Dream them.

Ellida   I've spent the last six years planning this book.

Heath   And you finally wrote!

Ellida   I did.

Edward   I'm so proud of you.

Ellida   Thank you, my love.

Edward   We have an appointment, Heath.

Heath   You got my results then?

Edward   They should be there when I log in. Why don't you head down and tell Liliana I'm on my way.

Ellida   Don't be rude, Edward, you can walk him down.

Edward   I was hoping to talk to you.

Ellida   You have an appointment.

Edward   I was trying to talk to you all weekend too. But there was always someone around. Almost as if you were choreographing it. Heath, please.

Ellida   Stay where you are, Heath.

Edward   Okay then. In front of Heath. You slept in the spare room Friday night.

Ellida   You were snoring.

Edward   I'm sorry for that. You slept in the spare room and when I came into the bathroom in the morning you started singing loudly without interruption and then you'd made breakfast for Hilda and Asa and organised a day of vintage shopping with them and then dinner at the pub with the Finchleys and you even invited Asa so we –

Ellida   She was kindly being the designated driver.

Edward   – so we wouldn't be alone and then another night in the spare room and then Sunday and another day of appointments and meetings and a trip to town alone for you and then a third night in the spare room and this time I was clever so I set an alarm for 4 a.m. and came over to you so we'd wake up together but you were cleverer and do-si-doed over to the main bed when I fell asleep and I woke up alone again and you really are terrifically good at guarding your own space but Ellida what happened on Friday night –

Ellida   Heath, shall I walk you over to the office?

Heath   Um . . .

Ellida   Come on, Heath.

She pulls him with her.

Edward, *alone.*

Five

Heath I'm dying.

Hilda Oh.

Heath I'm fucking dying.

Hilda Okay um.

Heath I know this is weird but I really need a hug.

She hugs him. He starts crying. After a while, he pulls back, stares at her shoulder.

I think that's my snot.

Hilda Oh. That's okay.

Heath Thank God you were here. Were you just passing? Oh is that homework?

Hilda Um. Yep.

Heath Comparative literature. What should I do?

Hilda How do you mean?

Heath Amyotrophic lateral sclerosis. That's why I've been shaking. And why I have trouble speaking sometimes. It only gets worse. And I'm getting worse fast. Should I kill myself?

Hilda Please don't do that.

Heath I think I should kill myself. I don't have very loving parents. They'd probably ship me off into care. I don't think they intended to have a child. They've hinted as much. What am I saying, hinted? Boarding schools and summer camps and a credit card with a twenty grand limit, a flat on the other end of town when I turned eighteen and I wasn't the one who chose the location, they did. A dream come true for an independent teenager. I just wanted –

Hilda A hug?

Heath You're very good at them.

Hilda   Am I? I've not really practised.

Heath   I've never been in love.

Hilda   Haven't you?

Heath   I've never been to South America. I always wanted to go to Patagonia. I'm scared of being stuck. Trapped in a body that can't speak anymore. I'm scared of telling my mother and hearing the pause while she figures out the right way to express emotions she doesn't have. And my father sending me a text after a few days saying, 'You okay, champ?'

Hilda   Don't kill yourself. Not yet.

Heath   And I made the stupid mistake of becoming an atheist only a couple of years ago and now all I can imagine is blackness and a void. No sound, no image, nothing. An absence. Not even that. Not even . . . oh fuck . . .

Hilda   Do you want another hug?

Heath   Oh fuck . . . Oh fuck . . . Ohhh fuck . . .

Six

Ellie *has just woken up. She sees* **Edward**.

Ellida   No. Get away from me. GET AWAY FROM ME.

Edward   Ellie?

Ellida   LEAVE ME ALONE.

Edward *goes to leave.*

Ellida   Edward? Is that you?

Edward   Yes it's me. Jesus.

Ellida   Oh God. I'm sorry.

Edward   What the hell was that?

Ellida   Oh fuck.

Edward   Ellie?

Ellida   I need to tell you.

Edward   Okay.

Ellida   Can you get me some water?

Edward *goes.* **Ellida** *stares into the corner as if she can see someone watching her.* **Edward** *returns with a bottle of water.*

Ellida   I met him when I was fifteen.

Edward   Okay.

Ellida   Things weren't. Well. Things were shit at home. And. Dad had just died and Mum was drinking a lot and I thought fuck it. And I moved out. Into a sharehouse in Stockholm with a bunch of uni students and –

Edward   Hang on. You left home when you were –

Ellida   Fifteen. Yeah.

Edward   Why didn't I know that?

Ellida   And a couple of my housemates, they were going to protests regularly and –

Edward   Why didn't your mum tell me that?

Ellida   I'm getting there . . .

Edward   Protests. What kind of protests? Did you get involved?

Ellida   Environmental. Yes.

Edward   Yes you got involved?

Ellida   Yes.

Edward   And that's how you met this guy.

Ellida   We hitchhiked to Germany. There was an opencast mine, it had just flooded and it was poisoning a natural reserve nearby. We chained ourselves to the gates –

Edward   Ellie, that is –

Ellida   We were arrested on the third day. They put us in the back of a van and it stunk in there, I mean none of us had washed for days and it was the middle of summer and Finn made a joke about showers in prisons and I laughed and he looked me and it was the first time he'd really noticed me in three days and he asked me my name. I was barely able to open my mouth to say it, I was so nervous. He asked me if I was scared and I lied and said no. On the way to the police station he told me stories about other protests he'd been arrested at. One time they'd cut down a tree in the Amazon while he was still sleeping in it. When we got to the station they separated the women and the men and by the time I was released the next morning he'd already been transferred somewhere else. Over the next months I kept going to protests with the friends I'd made in Germany. Then we got a message from Finn on Facebook. Said he was organising a sit-in at a mine they were opening on Indigenous land in Australia. Told us to come along. Three of us found the cheapest tickets we could to Darwin. He was waiting for us in the car park of the airport in his ute and he hugged me and said 'I missed you, Ellida' and the feeling in my chest when he said that. We sat up late drinking around the fire that night and he was looking at me and smiling and I got a bit drunk and fell asleep on the ground next to the fire and in the morning I woke up and Sally, one of the two friends I'd travelled with, was coming out of Finn's tent. And then over the days it was a few different girls coming out of his tent but he kept smiling at me from the other side of the campfire in the evenings and that kept going on for a while until one day a group of us sabotaged the electrical substation at the mine.

Edward   You . . .

Ellida   We poured petrol over it and set it on fire.

Edward   Fucking . . .

Ellida   And Sally's arm caught on fire, she'd spilt some petrol on it, and she was screaming and the fire was spreading and the others were staring at her paralysed so I just kind of tackled her to the ground, and wrapped my jacket around her arm and the others told Finn what I'd done when we got back to camp and he came to me that night and told me how proud he was of me and –

Edward   Yeah.

Ellida   Fuck. There was this thing I used to do. When I was a girl in Mölle I used to love going swimming in autumn when the waves start getting really wild there. I used to dive under the water, down to where the undercurrents are strongest and I used to just. Let go. Let the power of the current take me wherever it wanted. Sometimes I ended hundreds of metres from shore, spit up near some rocks or slammed against the beach, but it always felt . . . like I belonged wherever I ended up . . . that's what it was like with Finn. When we had sex the first time and when we left the others eventually and bought a boat in Darwin and set out to sea together, it was like –

Edward   Just the two of you?

Ellida   Yes.

Edward   How old was he?

Ellida   What?

Edward   How old was Finn? Were you still fifteen?

Ellida   I was about to turn sixteen.

Edward   Fifteen. Right. And he was?

Ellida   I don't know. In his thirties.

Edward   Right.

Ellida   Please don't do that.

Edward   I'm not doing anything, Ellie.

Ellida   I'm trying to explain to you.

Edward   And I'm trying to understand.

Ellida   I'm happy with where I am. I'm happy that I'm here.

Edward   Are you?

Ellida   Yes. I thought so. I did. I mean. I wasn't lying to myself. Ed.

Edward   Yes?

Ellida   I wasn't lying to you.

Edward   Okay.

Ellida   I'm sorry.

Edward   What for?

Ellida   I thought that this was over.

Edward   What? What are you talking about?

Ellida   I don't want this to be happening to me.

Edward   What's happening to you?

Ellida   I see him.

Edward   What do you mean?

Ellida   He's watching me. He has this look in his eye.

Edward   Back then? The way he looked at you that night?

Ellida   No no. Now.

Edward   Right now?

Ellida   Whenever I wake up.

Edward   You see him?

Ellida   He's standing there looking at me. Waiting for me to wake up.

Edward   I'm sorry I was watching you sleep.

Ellida No you don't understand. It's happened before.

Edward Maybe we should get you back on the olanzapine, at least at nighttime –

Ellida THIS IS NOT. About medication. Ed. Did you hear me? It happened before.

Edward When?

Ellida That night I had the miscarriage. I woke up and he was sitting on the chair in the corner of the room. Smiling at me. I mean he was smiling but he was heartbroken and I felt this pain tearing through me and that was the beginning of –

Edward Ellie, this is ridiculous. You can't tell me that –

Ellida You have no idea what happened between us.

Edward Look. I get it. This man was important to you. That's become clear this past week. I'm surprised that I never knew anything about it, I know we agreed not to share everything, what did you call it? Delve too deeply, I get that but this, this seems like something that would have maybe been necessary information for me to –

Ellida I promised myself to him.

Edward What does that mean? This isn't a fucking Jane Austen novel, Ellida. Life happens. Things are complicated. You were in love with him. I get it. And it's okay. Look at me. It's okay. If you were more in love with him than you ever have been with me that's okay but –

Ellida I can't compare the two of you.

Edward What does that even mean? Promised yourself to him?

Ellida I was with him. That night on the oil rig.

Edward Stop.

Ellida Ed.

Edward   No. No. I don't want to hear this.

Ellida   You're the first person I've ever told this.

Edward   Then don't. Don't tell me.

Ellida   I killed someone, Ed.

Edward   No you didn't.

Ellida   I did.

Edward   Fucking hell. Ellida.

Ellida   I'm sorry.

Edward *moves away from her.*

Ellida   After a couple of years we'd ended up in Norway shadowing whaling ships. And then one morning Finn showed me an article about a drilling platform BP was opening in the North Sea. He came up with a plan. We made this huge sign, a tarpaulin that we were going to hang off the edge of the platform. We went the night before the official opening. The sea was wild. It took us hours to get out to the rig. We managed to moor against one of the pylons and climbed up. It was raining hard and the wind made it almost impossible to move. I tried to convince Finn to give up but either he couldn't hear me or . . . once we got to the top we started attaching the sign to the platform. I was busy tying off my end when I heard this man yelling over the wind. And suddenly this security guard was grabbing at me. I screamed as loud as I could and pushed him back and we both slipped and ended up on the floor. Finn saw us struggling and started running. Then the security guard had me in a lock and Finn got to us and he pulled him away and then they were hitting each other and I managed to get to my feet and I threw myself at the guard, I was just trying to get him to the ground but the wind must have been coming in the same direction and when I hit him, it was like he flew, like he flew away from me, he had this panicked look in his eyes as he flew back and he tried to right himself by the edge of the platform but he slipped and fell. Fell into the sea . . .

Edward   Jesus.

Ellida   We got back down to the boat and drove around trying to find him in the water but someone must have seen us on CCTV because suddenly the alarm was going off and Finn turned to me and said we had to leave. I was screaming at him, screaming while he drove us back to land and he didn't say anything, he just drove the boat through the storm until we got closer to shore and the weather was finally calmer and the sun was starting to come up behind us and he dropped anchor and he took me to the back of the boat. And he said go. Swim to shore. Get back home. Start again. And he said I'll come back to you. I promise.

Edward   Ellie.

Ellida   And I used to wear my father's wedding ring around my neck and I took it off and –

Edward   Ellie you were sixteen.

Ellida   I was seventeen by then.

Edward   You were a teenage girl.

Ellida   And I told him to give me one of his rings and I put it on the necklace with mine and I threw it into the sea, into the currents. We watched the rings sink into the sea.

Edward   This is. Ellie. This is –

Ellida   I promised to wait for him.

Edward   That is insane. That is completely. You know that right? We make promises as teenagers. No one in their right mind would ever expect you to keep those promises as an adult.

Ellida   He's coming for me. I know it.

Edward   He is not. Ellie. Look. With all due respect for your obvious terror in this moment, I really do think we should be re-examining the dosage of your SSRIs and consider maybe something stronger for the short term –

Ellida   No.

Edward   Just the short term.

Ellida   He is coming.

Edward   You're having hallucinations. You're seeing a man from twenty years ago.

Ellida   Yes.

Edward   And what? He's reminding you of your what, your pact? Your pact with the sea?

Ellida   Yes.

Edward   Are. You. Hearing yourself?

Ellida   Yes.

Edward   And you miscarried our child because of him? Because he was watching you?

Ellida   I think so, yes.

Edward   Fuck you.

Ellida   I'm sorry.

Edward   I mourned with you, Ellie. I had a little bit of me torn out too, not physically, I know, and I wasn't pumping blood and life into that child, I know that, and I never made a big deal of it because you were in so much fucking pain but that happened to me too. And it didn't fucking happen because you used to be in love with some crazy guy who has a thing for underage girls –

Ellida   That WASN'T –

Edward   There's no version of that story where what he did was appropriate let alone deserves to be called love but that's how you see it and I respect that but what I won't let you do is frame my unborn child's death as an act of revenge for you being unfaithful to –

Ellida   It was my fault. I should never have let it happen.

Edward   What? Getting pregnant with me? Oh my fucking. Okay. We should stop this conversation. Before the next ten things are said that can never be unsaid.

Ellida   Okay.

Edward   Ellie. Ellida. Miscarriages happen. They're incredibly common. They have medical explanations.

Ellida   I'm not a medical expert. But I know what happened to me.

Edward   Won't you at least try what I'm suggesting with –

Ellida   I don't want you to be prescribing me medication anymore.

Edward   Okay. We can find someone else to –

Ellida   I don't like that I've become dependent on chemicals to feel balanced.

Edward   Okay.

Ellida   I'm going to stop taking everything.

Edward   Ellida. That's really fucking –

Ellida   Ed.

Edward   Okay. If that's what you want. Okay.

Ellida   I'm sorry. I'm sorry for how hard this is for you. I'm trying.

Edward   Honey. I know. I know. I love you. You're safe here. Even if he comes. Which he won't.

Ellida   He will.

Edward   I'll fucking send him away. We'll get a restraining order if we have to. He won't get to you.

Ellida   Okay. You promise?

Edward   Of course. Oh God, you poor fucking thing. Come here.

They hold each other tightly.

Seven

Asa   So what, and then you kissed him? Tell me you kissed him.

Hilda   No we went straight to third base.

Asa   You did not.

Hilda   What is third base again.

Asa   Fuck you.

Ellida   What are you two doing in swimwear?

Asa   We're coming to the lake with you.

Ellida   Did your father put you up to that?

Hilda   Yes.

Asa   No.

Ellida   I'm looking forward to the company. I can show you my favourite spot.

Hilda   Oooh yay.

Asa   Hilda's got a boyfriend.

Hilda   No I don't.

Asa   Right. It's just a guy she randomly jacks off from time to time.

Ellida   Well, that sounds lovely.

Hilda   I hate you both.

Asa   She hasn't even kissed him yet. He's dying.

Ellida   Heath? You're in love with Heath?

Asa   She lay with him in the grass for hours while he cried on her.

Hilda   I'm going to push you off a cliff today.

Ellida   I think that's beautiful, Hilda.

They have exited.

Finn Marcet *enters. He sits at the table.*

After a while, the sound of **Ellida** *coming.*

Ellida   You guys go ahead, I forgot my sunglasses and my –

She sees him. She stops, paralysed.

Finn   Hey, El.

She takes in a sharp breath.

How you been?

Part Two

One

The same moment.

Finn Hey, El.

She takes in a sharp breath.

How you been?

She can't speak.

Quite hard to find your address. You changed your name.

Ellida Please don't . . .

Finn Wikström? Is that your mother's name? Never did get to meet your mother. I think we were just about to, weren't we? Go to Sweden and meet your mother. And then . . .

Ellida I'm sorry.

Finn We've got time to talk about it. This is . . . very different.

Ellida You could have written to me.

Finn I did. Few times. Wrote to your agents and your publishers. I read that book of yours.

Ellida I never got any message.

Finn So I looked you up in the company register. This address came up.

Ellida You read my book?

Finn Sounds like you had quite the time at university.

Ellida Sorry.

Finn Don't say that. There's nothing for you to say sorry for. You live here alone?

Ellida   No.

Finn   I'm glad you went to uni. I'm glad it didn't fuck you up.

Ellida   Finn.

Finn   We've got time to talk about it. It's not where I imagined you. This place.

Ellida   It's my husband's.

Finn   You married?

Ellida   Finn . . .

Finn   You got married?

Ellida   You should go.

Finn   Why d'you get married?

Ellida   He might come back. Any moment and –

Finn   Hang on. El. Wait. It's okay. I'll talk to him.

Ellida   No, you can't do that. Finn please –

Finn   Did they not tell you what prison I was in?

Ellida   What?

Finn   I asked my lawyer to send you a letter. To the address in Stockholm. When I went in. To tell you where to visit me.

Ellida   I wasn't living in Stockholm. I was back in Mölle. And then by the time you were sentenced I was in Cambridge.

Finn   You didn't want to find out where I was?

Ellida   I thought about it. A lot.

Finn   Probably easier. For both of us. That way.

Ellida   I can meet you in town. I can meet you at the café in town. But please leave.

Finn   I was worried you'd look different. But you don't. You look exactly the same.

Ellida   That's not true.

Finn   I missed you, El.

Ellida   Finn . . .

Finn   It's over now. We can breathe.

Ellida   Please don't.

Finn   We've got time.

Ellida   Finn, this can't –

Edward   Ellida? Are you out there?

Ellida   GO. Go please. Just go. I'll meet you wherever you want but –

Edward   Ellida, you need to move your car, there's a delivery van that –

He sees **Finn**.

Edward   Who's that?

Neither answers.

Who are you?

Finn   Is that your husband?

Ellida   Yes.

Edward   Yes I am her husband. Who are you?

Finn   How long you been married?

Edward   Excuse me?

Ellida   Edward. It's him.

Edward   Him? You're . . .

Finn   So she told you about me?

Edward   You're Finn.

Finn   I am. How long you been married to El?

Edward   You're going to need to leave. Otherwise I'll –

Finn   I remember what you said to me, El. I haven't forgotten that morning. Out at sea.

Ellida   Please don't –

Edward   I can order you a taxi if you like. The station's not far and you can –

Finn   Have you forgotten what you said, El?

Ellida   No, but –

Edward   Stop this. Stop talking to her. You have no right to –

Finn   What's that?

Edward   You're a fucking psychopath. How did you even find us?

Ellida   Ed, stop.

Edward   This is private property. This is private property and you don't have permission to be here. If I need to call the police –

Ellida   EDWARD.

Edward   If you want to contact us. My lawyers are based in Manchester. I'll write their contact down.

Finn   El and I have things to discuss.

Edward   No you don't. And you won't.

Finn   You can't stop me from talking to –

Ellida   I'll meet you somewhere else but please –

Edward   No you won't. I don't mind calling the police, Ellida –

Ellida   We are NOT calling the –

Finn   Call them. If you want.

Edward   And maybe you can explain to them what you were doing fucking a fifteen-year-old girl in 2005.

Ellida   STOP THIS.

Finn   It's okay. I'll leave. I'll come back here tomorrow night. At ten o'clock.

Edward   Is this guy fucking? Look at me. If you come. I will have people waiting for you.

Finn   Is that what you want, Ellida?

Ellida   No.

Finn   Will you meet me alone?

Edward   No she won't.

Finn   Ellida?

Ellida   I need to think.

Finn   I'm leaving now. I'll be back tomorrow.

Edward   Don't you –

Finn   See you tomorrow, El.

He's gone.

Silence.

Edward   Ellida. Please make this stop.

She walks off in a daze.

Two

Hilda   We want a second opinion.

Edward   You want a what?

Hilda   A second opinion. We feel –

Edward   Excuse me who is we?

Hilda   Heath asked me to help him communicate his feelings about –

Edward   Did you, Heath?

Heath   Well, I –

Edward   Ask Hilda to help?

Hilda   Yes he did. He finds communicating his –

Edward   A second opinion? Not a lot of neurologists around here.

Hilda   Don't you have a friend in Edinburgh?

Edward   I do, Hilda. You can go to my friend in Edinburgh, Heath. He'll give you a second opinion.

Hilda   I'll come with you to Edinburgh.

Edward   Ah. There's the catch. Unfortunately Hilda has exams in a month, Heath, she won't be able to accompany you to –

Hilda   Don't be a dick, Dad.

Edward   Apparently caring about my daughter's academic success is indicative of me being a penis.

Hilda   Stop it, Dad.

Edward   Hilda seems to have forgotten that she's seventeen and still under her father's legal –

Heath   I can go to Edinburgh on my own.

Hilda   No you can't.

Edward   You know I really do hope I'm wrong, Heath, though I doubt I am unfortunately –

Hilda   Dad, that's arrogant.

Edward   Wow. You do know I'm one of the UK's leading –

Hilda   This again.

Edward   Again? Jesus.

Hilda   Dad. Calm down.

Edward   I am calm, Hilda. I'm perfectly calm.

Hilda   Then why are you saying 'Hilda' like that?

Edward   Hilda.

Hilda   Yeah like that.

Heath   Hilda.

Edward   I thought you wanted Heath to be dying, Hilda?

Hilda   Dad.

Edward   And if I'm such an arrogant incompetent doctor and my gnoses are completely off the mark, see what I did there Heath, then you may very well be in the disappointing position of having a healthy boyfriend –

Hilda   Dad, please.

Edward   No hospital visits then, Hilda. You may have to resort to Munchausen by proxy to get your kicks –

Hilda   Stop it now.

Edward   'I really hope he's dying'. Is that not what you said?

Hilda   You asshole.

Heath   Hilda, it's okay.

Hilda   YOU FUCKING ASSHOLE.

Three

Asa   Oh my fucking God. New York is so cool. Have you ever been to New York, Dad?

Edward   New York? I don't think so.

Asa   Don't think so. I think you'd remember New York.

Edward   I went to a conference in New Jersey once. I think I saw Manhattan from a distance.

Asa   Didn't Mum always want to go to New York?

Edward   We never made it.

Asa   That's shit.

Edward   Yes it is.

Asa   Are you okay, Dad?

Edward   Why are you googling New York? Planning a trip?

Asa   Um. Shit. You're not in a great mood are you?

Edward   What does that mean?

Asa   I'll tell you when you're happy again.

Edward   Tell me what?

Asa   Trust me, Dad, let's wait.

Edward   Fucking tell me. What's wrong with you?

Asa   Alright, F-bomb.

Edward   What's going on, Asa?

Asa   I need you to calm down.

Edward   What is it with the two of you?

Asa   The two of us? What did Hilda do?

Edward   You know part of growing up is realising that your parents are flawed.

Asa   Oh believe me. Lesson good and learnt. A long time ago.

Edward   And sometimes I won't be calm. Even if you want me to be.

Asa   But I, as a fellow grown-up, can choose not to impart information when said calmness is not extant.

Edward   You know that being smart is not always enough?

Asa   Right.

Edward   There are other qualities. Tact and sensitivity, reading the fucking room from time to time maybe and –

Asa   What have I done?

Edward   WHY ARE YOU GOOGLING NEW YORK?

Asa   Jesus.

Edward   It was a simple question. Why do we always have to get into the semantics?

Asa   I was playing. I was having a –

Edward   I'm sorry. I don't have a sense of humour right now.

Asa   I can see that.

Edward   ASA. Tell me.

Asa   I'm going to Yale. To do a PhD

Edward   Yale in America, Yale?

Asa   Yes.

Edward   How long for?

Asa   Five years. And maybe I'll stay.

Edward   I have my practice here. I'm nowhere near retiring.

Asa   I know that.

Edward   I can't just up sticks and move to America.

Asa   I don't want you to.

Edward   And what's Hilda going to do?

Asa   She can stay here.

Edward   Not without me.

Asa   You're staying here.

Edward   I could get in touch with some colleagues, see if there's any residencies available in New Haven. It's New Haven, isn't it?

Asa   No. Stop. I don't want you to come.

Edward   Hilda'll have to pull her finger out if she's going to apply to a US college.

Asa   You're not coming. I want to do this alone.

Edward   . . .

Asa   It's nothing against you. Seriously. You're a great dad.

Edward   Why are you doing this?

Asa   Because I need some space. And I feel like I can't really process everything that's happened if I stay here.

Edward   You don't need to stay here. But there's perfectly good universities in Britain.

Asa   But then you'll be visiting me all the time.

Edward   So what? Now I'm not allowed to visit?

Asa   No please don't.

Edward   Excuse me?

Asa   Not for a while. I'll email you when I'm ready.

Edward   What the fuck did I do?

Asa   You didn't do anything.

Edward   Then why am I not allowed to visit?

Asa   This is not healthy.

Edward   Loving my daughter isn't healthy?

Asa   Dad, give me a hug.

He doesn't. He walks away.

Four

Ellida   I need you to leave the house tonight.

Edward   I'm not doing that.

Ellida   I tried to get him to meet me somewhere else. But he won't.

Edward   I'm not leaving.

Ellida   He's coming here. In less than two hours.

Edward   I am not leaving my own house. The house I brought up my children in. The house I lived in with my dead wife. I am not leaving it so you can –

Ellida   I'm sorry.

Edward   I think you've gone mad.

Ellida   Oh God.

Edward   I do.

Ellida   I can't make this go away, Ed.

Edward   I need you to hear me when I say this isn't normal behaviour. What you're asking, what you think is fair to expect of me –

Ellida   I don't expect anything of you.

Edward   What? Ellida, you just asked me to leave the house so you can –

Ellida   And I don't think it's fair. And I'm not asking, I'm begging. And I know you want to say no but –

Edward   If you pursue this path, this path you think you have to walk down, you'll lose all connection to –

Ellida   Maybe I need to lose connection.

Edward   To sanity? To decency. To kindness?

Ellida   I know this isn't decent. Or sane. Or kind. But I owe something to Finn.

Edward   Don't you fucking say his name. I don't want to hear his name. I don't want to –

Ellida   Everything was cut off. In a single second. Finn was every waking minute for me, he was the first thing and the last thing. Like I was breathing him and dreaming him and every move I made was towards Finn or away from Finn but Finn was the centre.

Edward   STOP SAYING HIS FUCKING NAME

Ellida   And then he was gone. And I lost my centre. And ever since then –

Edward   You've been unhappy since then? Because I've seen you happy, Ellida. When we moved here. You were fucking happy. That wasn't a lie. You can't tell me that was a lie.

Ellida   But underneath it.

Edward   NO. BULLSHIT. YOU WERE HAPPY.

Ellida   Please don't raise your voice like that.

Edward   No. I'm shouting. I want to shout and I'm shouting.

Ellida   Okay.

Edward   When we moved here you were happy.

Ellida   But it didn't last.

Edward   Because you had a miscarriage.

Ellida   Because of Finn.

Edward   BULLSHIT.

Ellida   Stop it. Stop it. Stop it. Please stop this. Who are you becoming? I don't recognise you.

Edward   Well, guess the fuck what.

Ellida   You don't recognise me either.

Edward   I want my wife back. I want the Ellida that I met back.

Ellida   This is the Ellida that you met.

Edward   So it's my fault? For not noticing you were still in love with another man?

Ellida   Don't make this about fault. Nobody's done anything wrong.

Edward   Because you did a pretty good job of making yourself look like you were falling in love with me. I mean it certainly looked like there was nothing else on your mind. Those first nights –

Ellida   I wasn't pretending.

Edward   Well, which one is it?

Ellida   Part of me, part of me I didn't even know about, that part of me was, yes, it was lying to you. Or hiding something from you. Part of me was hiding something from myself. Ed. I was totally. I was shocked. I was. Two weeks ago . . . when I heard Finn's . . . when I heard his name again . . . I'd forgotten . . . I'd really forgotten until then –

Edward   Must have been really fucking important if you spent twenty years not thinking of him.

Ellida   There's no point in trying to explain this to you, I can't find the right words –

Edward   Everything was cut off for me too. I lost my centre too. I know what that's like. You don't have to explain that to me. But you know what, Ellie? Things end, they fucking disappear and you can't bring them back.

Ellida   Finn's not dead. He came back.

Edward   What you want to do. Is destroy everything. Your whole life. You want to destroy it.

Ellida   We didn't finish. It was cut –

Edward   And I won't let that happen. I have a responsibility to you, to stop you from doing this. It's madness. It's pure and utter fucking –

Ellida   I need to know how it would have ended.

Edward   I'm not leaving.

Ellida   Lyle is coming. He's taking you and the girls out to dinner.

Edward   Excuse me, you fucking enlisted Lyle to –

Ellida   He doesn't know about Finn. He just knows I need a night off.

Edward   A night off.

Ellida   I can't do what I need to. If you're here.

Edward   Do what you need to?

Ellida   . . .

Edward   Are you going to fuck him?

Ellida   Edward . . .

Edward   Oh fuck . . .

He tries to shake the thought loose.

I don't want to be doing this. I don't want to be fucking –

Ellida   Edward, please.

Edward   I know I'm a clichéd fucking controlling fucking pseudo-alpha cunt that wants his wife not to be about to fuck another fucking dude. WHAT A CUNT. LISTEN TO THIS CUNT AND HIS FUCKING DEMANDS. I want you to be my wife. I want you to be mine. Not anyone else's. I know. How fucking primitive of me.

Ellida   Jesus.

Edward   Oh Jesus fucking I can't get out of this, I don't know which way to turn I wish I could just smack my head open against that wall and obliterate these thoughts, these thoughts are going to fucking –

Ellida   Ed . . .

Hilda   Dad?

Edward   I can't be your father right now.

Ellida   You should go. I'll deal with this.

Hilda   Is he okay?

Edward   No. No. I'm not. I'm really not. Listen to Ellida.

Ellida   Just go. He'll be okay.

Hilda   Dad?

Edward   I can't.

Hilda *goes. Silence.*

Edward   When I was at that research institute in Turin that summer and I drove to pick you up at the Naples airport to take you to Amalfi. I spent the night in the hills in Umbria on the way. I went to this restaurant. Alone. And there was a woman dining alone too and the restaurant was full and the old lady running the restaurant, she insisted that the woman and I sit together. I was just planning on having a quick pasta while reading the newspaper, get up early, drive south, meet your flight. And there I was suddenly stuck having a three-course dinner with a stranger and then we were talking and she was cycling all the way from Russia to Africa and that impressed me and she was listening to science podcasts during her rides and she knew a lot about neuroscience for a layperson and it was a really pleasant evening, unexpectedly pleasant and then I noticed she was beautiful too and you and I were still fairly new, not married yet, still desperate to tear each other's clothes off the

moment we saw each other, pining when we were apart but
for a few hours this woman was with me and I could see in
the way she looked at me that she was waiting for me to ask
her back to my hotel and now I think back to that and –

Ellida   You regret not doing it?

Edward   My ego, my shitty ego, the tit-for-tat part of me,
yeah it wishes I could have had the moral ambivalence to –

Ellida   What I'm feeling is not ambivalence, Edward.

Edward   No I don't. I don't regret it. And all the drunken
advances at conference parties. And the phone numbers
snuck into my jacket pocket. And all the awkward
possibilities, they meant nothing at all, no matter how small
or lost I felt when things were difficult between us, because I
only ever wanted you. From the moment I met you. And you
can't say that, can you, Ellie?

Ellida   . . .

Edward   No you can't, Ellie.

Ellida   . . .

Edward   I'll take the girls out to see Lyle. I'll stay at the
hotel. I can't stop you. Or convince you. I don't want to be
who I can feel myself becoming. And I feel as if you didn't
really give me any choice in the matter. And I want to
fucking hate you for that. I wish I could feel a rage huge
enough and dark enough to see you and want to hurt you
but I can't rustle it up. It's not there. It's not there. And all
the shouts and threats and words and insults and petty
fucking . . . they're all empty, Ellie . . . I'm empty . . .

Ellida   Ed . . .

He shakes his head at her and goes.

Five

Asa   What happened to Edward?

Ellida   Your father's going to meet you at the hotel for dinner. Lyle's coming from Manchester.

Asa   Hilda said he was flipping out.

Hilda   He was totally flipping out, he said he wasn't my father.

Ellida   He didn't say that, Hilda, and he didn't mean it.

Asa   What did you do?

Hilda   Dad's been acting like a complete fuckwit.

Asa   Ellida? What did you do?

Ellida   There's someone I used to be with. He's come to visit.

Asa   Be with? Like sexually?

Hilda   Ugh. Asa. Gross.

Ellida   Yes.

Asa   Like a boyfriend?

Ellida   Yes.

Asa   When you were younger.

Ellida   When I was Hilda's age.

Asa   Oh my God. Blast from the past.

Ellida   Yeah.

Asa   And he's come to visit. And Dad's jealous.

Ellida   Something along those lines.

Asa   Is he staying here?

Ellida   No but he's visiting me tonight.

Asa   And Dad doesn't want you to.

Ellida   No.

Asa   Scandalous.

Hilda   You're sending Dad out to dinner so you can hang out with another man?

Ellida   Hilda, it's more complicated than –

Hilda   That's full-on cow behaviour.

Asa   Hey, Hilly.

Hilda   That's fucking off, Ellida. No wonder he's going crazy.

Ellida   I wasn't able to see him for a long time. For half my life. And now I can.

Hilda   You don't have to do things just because you can. I mean I learnt that when I was twelve.

Ellida   I don't want to talk about this anymore.

Asa   Hilda. She said it's complicated. Maybe we don't understand.

Hilda   And why couldn't you see him for half your life? Did he ride off on his horse and go to war? Was he busy besieging the city of Troy and then got lost on the way back with some Sirens?

Ellida   Kind of.

Asa   So you have been paying attention in Literature, Hilda.

Hilda   Fuck off.

Ellida   He was in prison.

Hilda   Oh so he's a criminal.

Ellida   No.

Hilda   They don't send innocent people to jail.

Asa   Um. Hilda. Yes they do.

Hilda   You're meeting an ex-con tonight? Here, out our place? And we're going to dinner so you can? Why is Dad okay with that?

Ellida   He's not.

Hilda   Why is Dad letting that happen?

Ellida   Because I asked.

Hilda   Why isn't he fighting back?

Asa   Because he's not that kind of guy. And that's good. Hilda, please calm down.

Hilda   Well, this is great news. Dad's a coward. And you're a cunt.

Asa   Get in the car. NOW.

Hilda   Thanks, Mum. I'm going.

She goes.

Asa   Were you in love with him?

Ellida   Yeah.

Asa   More in love than with Dad?

Ellida   At the time, yeah.

Asa   Fuck.

Ellida   I'm sorry.

Asa   Don't say sorry. Those are your feelings. You can't fix it. It just is what it is and it's a real fucking dilemma. And you're very confused. Are you sleeping?

Ellida   Not much.

Asa   You need to sleep.

Ellida   I know. I'm trying.

Asa   You need to meet him.

Ellida   I know.

Asa   You'll just have to deal with Edward hating you.

Ellida   I hate this so fucking much.

Asa   I know.

Ellida   I tried to make it go away. I tried to find another way out. I wish I could just erase that part of my brain. I wish I could go back to that summer my father died and not leave home, not go searching, not find myself fucking –

Asa   But you can't. And you'll figure out how to own it. And it made you who you are, Ellida. And against the yardstick of average human coolness you land somewhere just beyond uncool, maybe even slightly cool, maybe in the ranges of cooler than average –

Ellida   I'm sorry.

Asa   Don't fucking say that.

Ellida   How did you get so wise?

Asa   I didn't. I'm just faking it. Fake 'til you make it. Got me quite far, let me tell you. Hey, Ellie.

Ellida   Yeah.

Asa   You'll figure it out.

Six

Hilda   Don't you want to get out of the rain?

Heath   Is it still raining? I hadn't noticed.

Hilda   Did you just reference *Four Weddings and a Funeral*?

Heath   Terrific film. Terrible line. I bet those fuckers broke their promise and got married anyway. And then Hugh Grant probably cheated on her.

Hilda   More like Andie MacDowell cheats on him. There's definitely an ugly divorce.

Heath   Better an ugly divorce than a sociopathic marriage.

Hilda   I want to run away. Will you run away with me? Let's go to Patagonia.

Heath   I'd be charged with kidnapping.

Hilda   I'm eighteen in less than two months. Then we can go.

Heath   Your family's alright.

Hilda   No they're not. They're insane.

Heath   So are you. So am I. I don't think I ever once heard my mother screaming. Maybe once when I was about to walk on the Persian rug after I'd been playing in the garden. And my dad was mostly away or drinking scotch in his library and listening to Chopin. I saw him smile twice. Once when his team won the Americas Cup and once when he completed a hostile takeover of a former friend's bank. Never once at me. I'd prefer bat-shit crazy to robotic any day. It feels like I'm alive. Around you guys. You're fighting and the blood and the spit are flying and and it's energising –

Hilda   What if everything goes really bad? I mean worse than bad. Like irreversibly awful?

Heath   There is no such thing. Not that your dad or Ellida or Asa are capable of. Even if they do their very worst they'll still be human and full of love and fuck, Hilda, what you said about me –

Hilda   That wasn't –

Heath   Don't. It sounded exactly like something you'd say or feel even if you didn't say it. That's what I like about you.

Of course you like it that I'm dying. I was always a blip on the radar. Not even that. A foggy little nothing. A nobody. I studied the greats. I worshipped at the temple of greatness. And knew I'd never end up in that pantheon. I still won't. But dying has made me briefly cool.

Hilda   Don't say that.

Heath   You'd never have looked at me twice if you didn't know –

Hilda   Well, you are hot.

Heath   That was always the enigma with me. My mother said it to me once when she came home drunk from a party and I was on the couch watching a Tarkovsky film at 1 a.m. 'How can you be so beautiful and yet so entirely uncharismatic? Do at least try to develop a personality, darling.'

Hilda   She did not say that.

Heath   Her exact words. And I get it. There was no fire in me. No scream. No libido.

Hilda   Really?

Heath   No. None. I liked listening to Allegri's *Miserere* in various cathedrals and comparing the acoustics. I'm the guy who signed up for the art restoration workshops that the Louvre put on, six months early. I bought a broken Stradivarius and repaired it. That made me cry and leap with joy, seriously I leapt with joy when I won the violin at the auction. I had deep deep emotion about everything apart from this.

He hits his chest. Harder and harder. **Hilda** *takes his hands, stops him.*

Hilda   What about now?

Heath   Now I'm confused. It's like I have a body for the first time in my life and it's because it's failing.

Hilda   It hasn't failed yet.

Heath   And all of these urges they seem foreign to me. They're in me but they're strangers. Strange flowing longing things. And I can't watch a movie anymore I can't concentrate. I can't read a book. I really want to kiss you, Hilda.

Hilda   Then kiss me.

Heath   I can't. I can't.

Hilda   Yes you can.

Heath   I found the scream. The scream has arrived. And it's urging me to do crazy unhinged things like –

Hilda *kisses him. He breaks free gently.*

Heath   Your father is going to kill me.

Hilda   Cheaper than Dignitas.

Heath   Oh my fucking God you are dark.

Hilda   I looked it up. And second cousins is genetically negligible so the number of times we're removed . . . And your lot has been stuck in Cornwall all these years –

Heath   What did you google? Can I kiss my fourth cousin?

Hilda   Yep.

Heath   Bet you lit upon some interesting Reddit threads.

Hilda   Oh my God. They say distant cousins even have an increased chance of successful reproduction.

Heath   Oh my God. We are not. You are not. Jesus, Hilda.

Hilda   Okay. That wasn't what I was suggesting. But okay. Thanks for the emphatic response.

Heath   No, I mean –

Hilda   I was just quoting interesting tidbits from the fucking medical fucking FUCK YOU.

Heath   Hilda . . .

Hilda   Don't look at me like that. I'm sorry I kissed you. Oh my God I am so –

Heath   No please, Hilda –

She's gone.

Seven

Finn   You were hoping I wouldn't come.

Ellida   Yes.

Finn   I said I would.

Ellida   I know.

Finn   I keep my promises.

Ellida   It's been twenty years.

Finn   And you forgot.

Ellida   Yes. No. Both.

Finn   I was on my own.

Ellida   I'm sorry.

Finn   No, I'm saying. I was on my own. And I only had one thing to think about.

Ellida   I'm sorry.

Finn   Getting out and getting back to you.

Ellida   I'm –

Finn   El. I said you don't need to say that. Look. If the situation had been reversed. If I'd had all these distractions. I mean life is good. Life out here is really good. And when I was inside I realised that, I hadn't realised that, El, I was too busy, I was on a track and I . . . El. I meant what I said. I'm glad you're happy.

Ellida   I'm not.

Finn   Because of me?

Ellida   Why did you insist on meeting me here?

Finn   Because I didn't want you to make some rash decision. Without thinking it through. I wanted you to consider what you're losing if you –

Ellida   What I'm –

Finn   All of this, it's comfortable. It's beautiful. You've got attachments. Not easy to let go.

Ellida   What are you asking of me?

Finn   No. El. Only if you want it yourself. I'm not going to twist your arm.

Ellida   This is too fast.

Finn   All of this. Reckon you can leave it behind?

Ellida   I can't just –

Finn   Okay.

Ellida   Finn. I can't. I can't.

Finn   I found a boat. In Whitehaven. Fishing trawler, good bones.

Ellida   You're going back to –

Finn   Going to take her over to Dublin. Got a mate there, runs a dry dock. We should be able to fix her up in a month or so.

Ellida   I didn't think you'd want to –

Finn   Look at the world, El. Look at what they're doing to her. You might not notice it up here in paradise but –

Ellida   I'm in love with Ed.

Finn   Are you?

Ellida   I like my. My life is. Good.

Finn   I can see that.

Ellida   You and me. We don't know each other anymore.

Finn   Well, if you're in love with him. And the two of us are strangers. I've got my answer.

Ellida   Not strangers. We're not strangers.

Finn   I'm glad I saw you. After fifteen years. You start to wonder if you made it all up. Like you just invented a story in your dreams and it's become all you can hold on to so it has to become the truth, it did happen didn't it?

Ellida   Yes.

Finn   You were with me that night?

Ellida   Of course I was.

Finn   We didn't mean to do it, did we?

Ellida   You didn't do anything. You were just protecting me.

Finn   Right. I thought I made that up.

Ellida   I remember everything. Every split second of it.

Finn   The story I told to the police. To the investigators. To the lawyers. I told that story so many times. I deleted you. For years you were only up here. And mostly only when I was sleeping.

Ellida   I know you don't want me to say it. But I wish I could say sorry a million times. Finn, what you did for me –

Finn   Don't mention it.

Ellida   Is that a joke?

Finn   Yeah I've still got some jokes in there. Can't beat that out of me.

Ellida   Finn. Thank you. Thank you.

Finn   I wasn't going to let a young woman go to jail. And you didn't mean to kill him.

Ellida   We should never have gone that night.

Finn   Why d'you say that? It was a mistake. He shouldn't have grabbed you. He's the one who started it.

Ellida   We were trespassing.

Finn   No, El, that's groupthink, that's bullshit, you can't. Jesus, El, not you too. That's what they do. That's exactly what they rely on. They make the consequences so fucking severe and they call it a fucking deterrent, where's the fucking deterrent for fucking oil companies, a piddly fucking fine, a grain of sand in the fucking Sahara, El, that's how much they pay for killing us all, and jail time, forget about that, and we go to jail for a decade and a half for fucking trespassing.

Ellida   I killed a man.

Finn   That was an accident. And if the same thing had happened with a bouncer outside a bar in downtown London, I would have got off scot-free. You know how many times they mentioned our fucking sign in the court case? And on and on about my politics. BP made sure everyone else in the community knew exactly why I was going down and it sure as fuck wasn't because a working-class bloke from Yorkshire carked it. He was convenient. They couldn't believe their bloody luck that night. They made an example of me, El. And they'll keep doing it. Look at all those Just Stop Oil protesters recently. You think those sentences were fair? Big business doesn't like the fucking gall of us and they make sure their little puppets in government do the dirty work for them.

Ellida   I get why you're angry.

Finn   I'm not angry. I'm focused. I'm determined. And I'm getting back to it. Because it's war now. And there's no safe side.

Ellida Jesus.

Finn What?

Ellida I remember you.

Finn What, my rants?

Ellida Joking again.

He smiles.

I like your smile.

Finn Same smile.

Ellida Bit sadder.

Finn Na. Don't let the bastards get you down.

Ellida I don't know what to do, Finn.

Finn D'you remember Ellida back then?

Ellida What?

Finn Ellida. Back when she met me. You remember her?

Ellida I think so.

Finn What would she do?

Eight

Lyle You're scaring your daughters.

Edward Am I? How's that?

Lyle You're just sitting there, staring into the distance chewing slowly on your food. And when someone asks you a question you look at them, slight pause, smile, disconnected fucking horror film smile and 'it's okay'. Dude it's clearly not okay.

Edward I'm sorry, Lyle. I'm sorry, kids.

Lyle They're not here.

Edward   Aren't they?

Lyle   You're outside. Standing in the rain. Laughing.

Edward   Was I laughing? That's odd.

Lyle   Are you having a spontaneous psychotic episode?

Edward   The evidence would point in that direction.

Lyle   I'll give the girls some money and send them to the club.

Edward   There's a club in Ullswater? Like a dancing drugtaking-type club?

Lyle   Yes. I googled it.

Edward   Why have I never been there?

Lyle   You've been busy with a family.

Edward   Oh yes. Am I still laughing?

Lyle   Not really.

Edward   Jolly good. Fabulous. Fantastic. Splendid.

Lyle   What's happening?

Edward   She didn't tell you?

Lyle   Who's she?

Edward   Who do you think?

Lyle   You have lots of shes.

Edward   Maybe that's my problem.

Lyle   Don't become a misogynistic dick. Find a more original type of crazy.

Edward   Wow. Spouting the wisdom tonight aren't you? Where's the manchild gone?

Lyle   Kicked him to the kerb. Told him he was ruining my marriage prospects.

Edward   You getting married? Don't do it. Seriously don't fucking do it. Don't. Look at me. Lyle. Look at me. Don't do it.

Lyle   I got it. Thanks.

Edward   I got married because I was scared. Both times.

Lyle   You got married because you were in love.

Edward   Both times?

Lyle   Yes.

Edward   Everyone's leaving me.

Lyle   No they're not.

Edward   They are, they're fucking abandoning ship. I wasn't enough. For Aisha. Or for anyone else. Is it really that hard to be around me?

Lyle   I don't find you hard to be around.

Edward   I know I can be stern. I know I can be distant. I don't like feeling like things are falling apart, Lyle. So I force them all together and make them stick and squish things that don't fit into spaces that don't want them and the whole thing is collapsing now and everything I've been scared of since I was a fucking kid is happening to me, it's fucking crumbling and I had nightmares about this and they looked exactly like this exactly fucking like this –

Lyle   Hey. Dude. Dude. Look at me. Nothing is falling apart.

Edward   Yes it is.

Lyle   If you let Asa go. If you send her off with your blessings. If you don't bug her with WhatsApps and FaceTimes. If you wait. Like silent, supportive waiting, and be there whenever she calls you without resentment or snarkiness. Then she will miss you within months, a year at most. And she'll come home and you can wash her clothes and cook her a pie and hold her while she cries about her ex-girlfriend –

Edward   Girlfriend? What?

Lyle   Yep.

Edward   And how do you know about Yale?

Lyle   Because I don't make it about me.

Edward   You're not her fucking father.

Lyle   And neither will you be if you keep going on like this.

Edward   I'll always be her father.

Lyle   You can tell yourself that while you're drinking that six-pack alone on the porch with your dogs, listening to the races.

Edward   I'll never listen to the races.

Lyle   Hundred per cent. That's what happens to men who don't listen to their daughters. Next step after that is hip operations and a fentanyl addiction. Nothing is falling apart.

Edward   You don't know that.

Lyle   Hey. I have something for you. Come out of the rain.

Edward   No. I like it.

Lyle   I found this when I was packing up in London. It's Aisha's.

He pulls a t-shirt out of a plastic bag.

Edward   Why do you have Aisha's t-shirt?

Lyle   She left it at my place. Must have been like twenty-five years ago.

Edward   Why did she stay at your place?

Lyle   I think we'd been out in Shepherd's Bush and the tubes weren't running.

Edward   Did you fuck her?

Lyle   Dude.

Edward   Did you?

Lyle   Fuck off.

Edward   Answer the question.

Lyle   No. I didn't Edward.

Edward   Why not?

Lyle   Because you're my mate.

Edward   What does that matter? All's fair in love and war. She might have appreciated it.

Lyle   She spent the whole night talking about you.

Edward   Well, she's gone now so who gives a fuck?

Lyle   Take the t-shirt. And stop feeling sorry for yourself.

Edward   I'm feeling? What did you just?

Lyle   You heard me.

Edward *grabs him and pulls him into the rain.*

I want to hit you.

Lyle   Then do it. Fight me because you can't fight Ellida.

Edward   What did she tell you?

Lyle   Nothing.

Edward   Bullshit. You told her to meet him.

Lyle   Meet who? Who's she meeting?

Edward   Stop fucking lying to me.

Lyle   I'm giving you one week. If you're still a cunt after that, lose my number.

Edward   Get the fuck out of my face.

He disappears. **Hilda** *has been watching.*

Hilda   What's that?

Lyle   Let me get it.

Hilda *has walked into the rain to pick up the t-shirt.*

Hilda   What is it?

Lyle   Your mum's t-shirt.

Hilda   This is Mum's?

Lyle   Yes.

Hilda   She used to wear this?

Lyle   Yeah.

Hilda   When?

Lyle   When she was in her twenties. Maybe earlier. I mean it's –

Hilda   Tribe Called Quest. Is that a band?

Lyle   It's a very fucking cool rap group. I'll send you a playlist.

Hilda   He left it lying in the rain. He left Mum's t-shirt lying on the ground in the –

Lyle   Yeah's he's being a bit of a dick.

Hilda   This is all Ellida's fault.

Lyle   No. Being a dick is a choice. As the great Eleanor Roosevelt said, nobody can make you be a dick unless you choose to be a dick yourself.

Hilda   I wish he'd never met her.

Lyle   Whoa whoa whoa. I'm the one who introduced the two of them.

Hilda   Severely misjudged, Lyle.

Lyle   Just because they're going through a bit of a rough –

Hilda   She's still in love with her ex.

Lyle   She's what? What ex?

Hilda   And she's seeing him tonight.

Lyle   No that can't be.

Hilda   It's happening, Lyle. Right now.

Asa   Where did Dad go?

Hilda   He threw this on the ground. It's Mum's shirt. Lyle had it.

Lyle   I was packing up my flat in London and –

Asa   Holy shit. Tribe Called Quest. They're awesome.

Hilda   How do you know more about rap than me?

Asa   The only reason you know anything about rap is because I introduced you to it. Now I may not walk around dressed like Little Simz but that doesn't mean –

Hilda   I don't walk around dressed like –

Lyle   She's just baiting you.

Hilda   Shit.

Lyle   Asa has something to tell you, Hilda.

Asa   No. Not now. No no no no.

Lyle   You told me to say that when the three of us were alone.

Asa   I know but. Fuck.

Hilda   What is it?

Lyle   Asa's scared of saying it so she needs you to be nice.

Hilda   I'm not going to promise to be nice if it's something shit.

Asa   Oh my God. You see?

Lyle   It's not shit for Asa. So it should be not shit for you too.

Hilda   It sounds like it's going to be shit.

Asa   I'm going to America. For at least five years. I'll be back for holidays or maybe Dad will pay for you to visit me and we can go on a road trip, the falling leaves in autumn, they call it fall there, because of the leaves, and they really are breathtaking apparently –

Lyle   And stop. Let her react.

Hilda   Right.

Asa   Are you angry?

Hilda   No it's fine.

Asa   Are you being sarcastic?

Hilda   I'm looking forward to being the only black person in town. I mean I haven't felt weird enough these last ten years, being the only mixed-race family within miles, then the mixed-race kid of the mixed-race mum who gassed herself in a car at the local quarry, yeah one of those two poor black kids she left that poor white doctor all on his own with and yeah they can get a bit punchy at school can't they, let's say trouble adjusting shall we, maybe it's cultural the sudden aggression and floods of tears, or do you think it's genetic maybe, that younger one Hilda, why does she have a German name, I thought they were Nigerian? Yes that one Hilda does get in a funk and she is awfully prone to wearing black and I saw what looked like cut marks on her forearm the other day, we do really need to refer her to a white counsellor because the ethnic ones are in high demand and we only have one mixed-race kid in this district so she'll just have to make do with white woman wisdom and you know what? Most of the time that's fine. Most of the time that helps enough. But there used to be three of us and that was hard enough and then Mum fucked off and there were two of us for just one year before you left for uni but at least you came home a lot and this summer has been really important for me and now you're telling me –

Asa I'm sorry.

Hilda And do I wish you'd picked a better moment, any moment other than the night my father's marriage is falling apart, no, not at al, Lyle, that was a great shout, great shout, Lyle. And yes, Asa, I AM BEING SARCASTIC.

Lyle Night can't get any worse, was my thinking.

Hilda It just did. It just got much worse. Because now I'm not just going to be having the worst year of my life but I'm going to have to swallow all that and be ersatz wife number two for poor old Edward, now that Asa is vacating the post.

Asa I am not his –

Hilda Oh yes you fucking are. You do his washing. You cook dinner for him. You pay the overdue bills. You drive me to school.

Asa Because you're too lazy to get a licence, Hilda.

Hilda Which I could only afford to do because my ersatz mum –

Asa Stop saying the word ersatz as if you've studied Freud.

Hilda No this is good. Cut the umbilical cord. Walk on my own two feet. Grist for the mill, eh? What doesn't kill you straight away kills you in a slow painful way that leads to chronic pain and thoughts of despair, that's what they say isn't it? I'll be fine. Let's finish dinner.

Nine

Ellida I didn't plan this. Any of it. My mum told me to stay away from the protests. Not have anything to do with any of you. I was lost and I was glad to have someone to tell me

what to do. So I accepted her money and I moved to
England. I did my A levels here and somehow . . . I mean I
buried myself in study. I studied and studied and tried not
to think of you. And I got into Cambridge and everyone was
excited for me and that seemed like something I should care
about too and I let the enthusiasm carry me, I just floated
along and followed the obvious path and –

Finn   Married a doctor.

Ellida   That was afterwards. First I –

Finn   Did everything a university student does.

Ellida   The extreme version. Anything anyone else was
doing I did it twice as hard and three days longer. I wanted
to forget. And I succeeded. I lost years. I don't remember
half of it. The half I did ended up in my first book. And then
that took off and I was busy doing book tours and dating
semi-celebrities and living in Shoreditch and then the
second book wouldn't come and I was drinking too much
and reminding myself of Mum and I'd even spend weekends
with her in Mölle, we'd be drinking from the moment I
landed until the car picked me up to take me to the airport
three days later and then she died and I was in the US doing
book signings and I organised the funeral from afar but I
chose not to go back and I ended up in hospital on a stomach
pump in Las Vegas and my friend Lyle came to pick me up
and he introduced me to Edward and I was calm for a while.
And I had a family, maybe for the first time in my life. And
then I got pregnant and I saw you –

Finn   You were pregnant?

Ellida   I saw you watching me. Were you watching me?
Could you see me? Could you see I was pregnant?

Finn   You saw me? I'm so glad you saw me, El. I never knew.

Ellida   That last morning. I turned back while I was
swimming to shore. I just stood there, the water up to my
waist, and I watched the boat you were in become smaller

and smaller and I watched this little dot that was you leaving my life and I kept watching it until I couldn't differentiate the dot from the water anymore and it looked like you must have been swallowed up by the sea. And then you were the sea, the sea I was standing in, it was you, the waves and the salt and the sand between my toes, it was all you.

Finn   That's what we promised. El. Day after day in prison I remembered the words you said that morning and I remembered the sunrise and your soaked hair and your face covered in tears and the way you told me. The way your voice broke while you said it and the pain I felt hearing it and I kept that memory in the cupboard above the stove in the boat, remember the cupboard in the boat where you stuck that picture of your dad up, that's where I left it, and whenever I went to sleep I swam up to the boat, climbed up the ladder, down into the cabin, and into the kitchen. And you were standing next to the stove waiting for me with a cup of coffee the way you used to and you whispered it to me again, every night, I'll wait for you, every night, I went to sleep early so I could meet you there and hear you say it.

Ellida   How do I leave?

Finn   You let go.

Ellida   I'm scared.

Finn   Of course you are. It's fucking scary. But we've done scary before, El. Remember all the terrifying things we did without even blinking? Remember that, El? Like nothing could even touch us.

Ellida   Yeah I remember.

Finn   El.

Ellida   I want that feeling again.

Finn   Then let's fucking do it.

Ellida   Finn.

Finn   I want to hold you, El. Can I hold you?

Ellida   Oh shit.

Ten

Heath
My father was the keeper of the Eddystone Light
He courted a mermaid one fine night
From this union there came three
A porpoise and a porgy and the other was me
Yo-ho-ho the wind blows free
Oh, for a life on the rolling sea.

Edward   What are you singing?

Heath   It's a shanty.

Edward   You a shanty specialist?

Heath   That one's a local one. Good old Cornish classic. About a cannibal lighthouse keeper.

Edward   Ellida's father was a lighthouse keeper.

Heath   Did he eat his own children?

Edward   I don't think she had siblings. But maybe he ate them. Hadn't considered that.

Heath   I've been screaming at the sky.

Edward   That sounds fun. Let me have a go. FUCK YOU, ELLIDA. FUCK YOU, AISHA. FUUUUUCK YOOUU. Don't feel any better. What were you screaming?

Heath   TAKE ME. I'M READY.

Edward   Don't believe you.

Heath   OBLITERATE ME. COME ON. FUCKING STRIKE ME DOWN. I DON'T EVEN BELIEVE IN YOU.

Edward   We're standing too low. And it'll hit those electricity poles before it hits us. Maybe we could climb up them and try again.

Heath   Jesus Christ. You're just like your daughter.

Edward   That's the best compliment anyone's ever given me. I'm being a shit dad at the moment.

Heath   I think you've built up enough credits. I was thinking of throwing myself off a cliff tonight.

Edward   Ooh can I watch?

Heath   Didn't you swear a Hippocratic Oath or something?

Edward   Nah that's just bullshit. I can watch you kill yourself. Just don't tell anyone.

Heath   Very funny.

Edward   My wife, my first wife. The dead one. She did it in the local quarry. It's been abandoned for years. Kids shoot shitty TikTok videos there nowadays. Which as you can imagine is quite triggering for my daughters when a new one comes online. Aisha. That was her name.

Heath   Fuck you, Aisha.

Edward   Exactly. She was prepared. She bought a pipe and gaffer tape and routed the exhaust into the driver's seat window and taped all the openings shut and she must have turned the ignition on and just waited. She had a Frank Ocean album playing on repeat. That weekend I wanted to take everyone hiking in Scotland and the girls were moaning and Aisha had a cold but she insisted they go with me, she had a fight with Asa about it and then when she died of course Asa hated her even more for it and then it turned out she'd burned all of her possessions like anything she'd ever touched, clothes, bags, her fucking toothbrush, we found it all charred and melted in the firepit out the back and you know why I think she did it? Because we had a dog once named Daisy, a schizophrenic black labrador who almost killed Hilda so we put her down and Hilda thought it was her fault we were killing Daisy and she bawled and bawled when we took her to the vet and I'd forgotten to get rid of some of the spare collars and a leash and she found them every now and then in the months afterwards and she was inconsolable. So yeah Aisha fucked off and took everything with her and I've got nothing left to shout at and it doesn't even feel good shouting anymore do you have any drugs?

Heath   No.

Edward   I used to take a lot of drugs. I miss it.

Heath   Maybe I'll start taking drugs.

Edward   Do it. It's so fun. I'm not giving good advice tonight generally but that's the pearl of wisdom you should carry away from tonight's conversation.

Heath   I kissed Hilda. She kissed me. I'm much too old for her. And I'm dying and she's angry at me because I told her it's probably not a good idea. And I probably should have asked you first.

Edward   Ooh no that would be weird. Heath you are so old-fashioned. You really need to relax. Oh shit.

Heath   What happened?

Edward   Oh shit. Oh no. Oh no.

Ellida   No. Stop.

Edward   I'm thinking of her. I was trying not to think of her.

Eleven

Ellida   Stop. No. Jesus.

Finn   What happened?

Ellida   Did you know I was fifteen?

Finn   Wait what?

Ellida   Did you know?

Finn   This is what your husband was talking about.

Ellida   I was fifteen when I met you.

Finn   No.

Ellida   I was.

Finn   Why did you never tell me that?

Ellida   Did you not notice I was younger than the others?

Finn   All your friends were uni students, what the fuck were you –

Ellida   You couldn't tell?

Finn   What's that supposed to mean? Do you think I'm the kind of person that –

Ellida   I don't know. I don't know anything anymore –

Finn   Ellida. You told me you were eighteen. I heard you tell other people you were eighteen. We celebrated your nineteenth birthday.

Ellida   That was my sixteenth birthday.

Finn   Are you sure?

Ellida   Even if I was eighteen, I mean that's still young, how old were you?

Finn   How old was I?

Ellida   Yeah how old were you?

Finn   What's going on, El? What are you doing?

Ellida   I want to know how old you were.

Finn   I was. I don't know. Jesus. Thirty-two. Maybe thirty-three.

Ellida   I mean that's still fourteen, fifteen years –

Finn   I'm the same age as your fucking husband, Ellida.

Ellida   What was it about my vulnerability that –

Finn   You weren't vulnerable. You were tough, you were blowing up electricity plants, you were –

Ellida   I did that to impress you and yeah that's when you kissed me the first time –

Finn   Because it was impressive. I'm not supposed to be impressed by an eighteen-year-old, what am I supposed to check your fucking ID before I get feelings?

Ellida   Even if I was eighteen, even if I wasn't fifteen, which I was, even if, you saw that it all felt new to me, didn't you, you saw that I was discovering –

Finn   It felt new for me too. It felt like a discovery for me too. I remember crying in your arms once and you asking me what's wrong and me not knowing why I was crying but it felt so huge and I was scared of –

Ellida   I remember that.

Finn   I'm sorry. I'm sorry you were too young. I really didn't mean to fuck you up. I thought we were . . . It never felt unequal to me.

Ellida   But it was. And that's what I liked about it. I felt like I was learning so much and you didn't notice how awkward I felt or inexperienced or naïve –

Finn   No I didn't.

Ellida   And that made me feel invincible. But I just deleted those years, Finn. Those years I should have been screwing around with teenage boys or girls and going crazy and fucking up without consequences without –

Finn   Without killing someone.

Ellida   I'm old. In here. I feel like I've lived ten lives already. And I shouldn't be this old already.

Finn   You can start again.

Ellida   No. No. I can continue. Or swerve and take a different path but I can't go back. I took that from myself. Finn, I needed to meet you –

Finn   I needed to meet you too.

Ellida   I needed to meet you to finish this.

Finn   No.

Ellida   If that man hadn't died we would have had two more years maybe three, I can see it now, I would have grown away from you, towards my own life, I would have thanked you, for the belief, for the education, for the support and the love, I would have thanked you and said goodbye.

Finn   El.

Ellida   Goodbye.

Long silence.

Finn   I was worried about this. That you'd see me and be disappointed.

Ellida   This isn't about that.

Finn   No I get it. I watched myself grow gaunt and grey in the mirror. Lot of time to look in the mirror in prison.

Ellida   Please don't.

Finn   And yeah, you're right. It's easy to be impressive to a young woman. But you must have met quite a lot of impressive people since then and impressive doesn't cut it anymore.

Ellida   Don't.

Finn   It's alright. I told you. I got a boat. I'll be right.

She kisses him.

I'm going to go now. 'Bye, El.

She watches him go.

Epilogue

Lyle Morning.

Edward Morning.

Lyle What are you doing?

Edward What does it look like?

Lyle Like you're swimming laps in the hope of warding off a massive hangover. Did you sleep?

Edward I woke up on Heath's shoulder. You won't believe this but we went for a hike, I wanted to show him the closest bothy, it was one or two in the morning and we were using the torches on our phones and then his died and then mine died and we just cuddled up and went to sleep on the side of the hill. I slept on a heath on a heath.

Lyle Not one of your best.

Edward Before you ask I remember most of what I said to you last night.

Lyle And?

Edward Have I ceased being a cunt? Only time will tell.

Lyle How you feeling?

Edward Pretty shabby.

Lyle Where's Heath?

Edward He's inside making us breakfast.

Lyle Of course he is. You been inside?

Edward No. Went straight to the poolhouse and got my dookers.

Lyle What's your dookers?

Edward Scottish for cozzie.

Lyle   You scared of going in?

Edward *nods*.

Lyle   Do you know if she's in there?

Edward *shakes his head*.

Lyle   It's your house.

Edward   Kind of doesn't feel like it right now.

Lyle   That feeling will pass.

Edward   Who cares? I'll just sell it. Find somewhere else. Don't worry I'm not still going crazy. But this, all of this. It's not me, and it's not Aisha or Asa or Hilda. All of us. Will survive buildings and places and possessions. And they'll survive us.

Lyle   That's really convenient, Ed, because I was just looking for someone to be the first guest on my philosophy podcast.

Edward   Fuck off.

Lyle   You're not allowed to say that to me at the moment. You're in forgive-me-mode, Eddie. You have to ask me if I want a coffee and what kind of milk and let me eat all your bacon and laugh in amazement at all of my witty musings.

Edward   I'll do some of that.

Lyle   You will grow from this experience.

Edward   No I won't. I'll shrivel. I'll atrophy. I can feel it already.

Lyle   This may not be good news then.

Edward   What is it now?

Lyle   Hilda and I have been talking.

Edward   And?

Lyle   This is just for two terms.

Edward   What? What's for two terms?

Lyle   I've found a great school.

Edward   Manchester?

Lyle   You can come and visit on weekends.

Edward   You're visit martial are you?

Lyle   Yep.

Edward   And what she's living with you?

Lyle   I have an annex. But I won't let anyone visit her.

Edward   You can't even cook.

Lyle   I have a meal delivery service. It's very healthy. Dude, she needs to not be surrounded by old white dudes and their white offspring for a while. She needs a city and parties and art galleries and plays and everything a teenager needs to become an exciting adult and she watches Asa blossom and she wants that too and you need to let her do it.

Edward   I get that.

Lyle   And I know you're thinking of moving to Manchester too and you need to not do that. At least not until –

Edward   You can't stop me from moving to a city of my choice, Lyle.

Lyle   It would be a HUGE favour, Edward, if you don't move to Manchester until Hilda is ready for you to move there, and that may be never.

Edward   Great. Good plan. I'm going to buy a racing bike.

Lyle   Logical response.

Edward   Conquer a few massifs. You're right. My thighs will grow from this experience. If I die of a heart attack on Mont Ventoux it'll be your and Hilda's fault.

Heath   Grub's up, folks. Your larder is a joke, Ed, but –

Lyle   Are you going to let him talk about your larder like that?

Heath   Luckily I travel with my special assortment of chilli jams and hot sauces so do not despair. This chilli oil has crispy bits, cannot recommend it enough.

Edward   Ooh delicious.

Lyle   I gave you crispy chilli oil in that hamper from the farmers' market and you ridiculed me.

Edward   But I believe it when Heath does it.

Heath   Bacon of course, grilled mushrooms, avocado to spread, I truly hope neither of you have a thing against scrambled eggs because these bad boys are Michelin-level ova.

Lyle   You didn't call the eggs I'm about to eat ova.

Heath   Ovum. Ovaries. Ovulation. Triggering words for a man like you I imagine.

Lyle   Fuck me.

Heath   I know. I'm annoying. But I'll be dead soon.

Lyle   Good. I'm glad. Die quicker.

Edward   What is it with you?

Lyle   Because dicks like this dick ruined high school and university for me. Just effortlessly flagrantly intelligent and in a completely unnecessary way, as if they can't help but just soak up all knowledge just by floating past a book. Do you know how hard it is for a dyslexic dyspraxic dyscalculic motherfucker like me to remember a single important fact let alone a thousand, let alone enough to get him into med school let alone graduate, let alone with honours and becoming a surgeon, let me tell you how many nights I didn't sleep while I was –

Heath   You need to sleep. Learning doesn't bed in unless –

Lyle   Oh my God. Oh my God. I'm genuinely going to kill you.

Edward   I'm proud of you, Lyle.

Heath   Me too.

Lyle   I don't want either of you to be proud of me, I just want to find you irritating. Okay?

Heath   Okay. I figured out what my last sculpture is going to be. It will, effectively, be my first to be completely truthful.

Lyle   I don't care.

Edward   I do.

Lyle   You're just saying that because you're in guilt-mode. Guilt-free Edward wouldn't give a shit, Heath, just so you know.

Heath   You know the Belvedere palace in Vienna? You know how it has this massive green roof? Well, it didn't start like that.

Lyle   Copper. Oxidisation.

Heath   It started as sparkling bright orange metal. And it slowly corroded into muted green modesty . . . So . . . Seven sculptures. Monoliths, like that black thing at the beginning of *2001: A Space Odyssey*, but out of bright brand new copper. I'm going to build them up on a hill over a lake, like where we woke up this morning, Ed, seven next to each other, each with a slightly different layer of wax protecting it from the elements. I've figured out the timings. I've given the longest one two years to corrode, the shortest one year. And when I die. The sculpture that just turned green, that's where I'll get them to bury my ashes. I'm calling it The Seven Ages of Man.

Lyle   Whoa.

Edward   Shakespeare. *Twelfth Night*?

Heath   Close. *As You Like It*.

Lyle   Alright. That's actually pretty fucking cool.

Heath   Thank you, Lyle.

Lyle   Because it's not nauseatingly smart. It's got heart too. Good concept. Particularly because it involves you dying. Which I'm looking forward to.

Edward   Jesus.

Asa   Gooood morning.

Edward   What are you two doing up already?

Asa   I smelt bacon.

Hilda   Then she elbowed me in the ribs and said, bacon.

Edward   Did you guys sleep together? That's so cute.

Lyle   Wow. Of the five people here, I'm the only one who slept alone last night.

Edward   I slept on a heath on a heath.

Lyle   Oh for fuck's sake give it a rest.

Edward   I woke up in Heath's arms. Don't be jealous, Hilda.

Hilda   Why would I be jealous?

Heath   I told him I kissed you.

Hilda   Okay I'm leaving.

Edward   No no no no no. Sit down. Eat breakfast. I promise, I won't say anything else. Not even about Manchester.

Hilda   How does he already know about Manchester? Lyle, you are so bad at timing.

Lyle   He's fine. He's grown up.

Edward   I'm sorry that I've been a massive asshole, Hills. You deserve better.

Hilda   Thank you. I'm still moving to Manchester.

Edward   I wasn't expecting to sway you. No, that will be a much longer campaign. But I will persist.

Hilda   I'm moving to Manchester.

Edward   And I will support that. While looking on Rightmove every day for my own place.

Asa   Thank God he's fixated on Manchester instead of New Haven.

Hilda   Yeah that's right, Dad, why don't you move to New Haven?

Asa   Much easier to set up another practice in the UK. American bureaucracy's way too –

Lyle   He's not stalking either of you. He's going to be a happy empty-nester going for long rides and discovering new cafés in far-flung places and posting annoying photos of coffee art on Instagram. He'll be fine. Won't you, Ed?

Edward   Yes, boss. How do you like your coffee again? Oat milk?

Lyle   Oat milk, Edward, well remembered.

Edward *is on his way in when he runs into* **Ellida** *coming out. She has a suitcase and a travel bag with her.*

Edward   Oh.

Ellida   Hi.

Edward   I was just going to make coffee.

Ellida   Oh okay.

Edward   Do you have time? Are you leaving?

Ellida   I can wait.

Edward   You want one?

Ellida   I'm okay.

Edward   I'll be right back.

Hilda   Are you leaving?

Ellida   Yes.

Hilda   For long?

Ellida   I don't know.

Hilda   I'm moving to Manchester.

Ellida   Wow.

Hilda   Can I FaceTime you?

Ellida   Uh . . .

Hilda   It's okay if you don't want to.

Ellida   No I'm just surprised. Of course I'd love to FaceTime you.

Asa   I do voicenotes. I don't do face stuff. I'll send you voice notes.

Ellida   Appreciate the boundaries.

Asa   Just a warning. If you don't answer within twenty-four hours I get mortally offended.

Ellida   Noted.

Asa   Have a fun. Holiday. Or whatever this is.

Edward *reappears.*

Ellida   Guys, can I? Sorry, can Ed and I have a moment alone?

Lyle   Of course. Guys, skedaddle. Always wanted to say that. Skedaddle, peeps. Call me, okay?

Ellida   Say hi to Susannah for me.

Lyle   Oh um. It's actually Gertrude now. I'll tell you all about it. Or not. Or not.

They're all gone.

Ellida   You look different.

Edward   Do I?

He looks at her and smiles.

Ellida   Why are you smiling?

Edward   I don't know.

Ellida   Do you want to know what happened?

Edward   No.

Pause.

Are you leaving with him?

Ellida   No.

Edward   Do you need me to order you a taxi?

Ellida   I've got one arriving in a second.

Edward   Oh, well –

Ellida   I already texted the driver that he might have to wait.

Pause.

When I was twelve and my dad had his particularly theatrical mid-life crisis and sold his very successful business and applied for the position of lighthouse-keeper in Mölle, we were suddenly in the middle of nowhere in this little house, all alone together, and Mum hated Dad for taking her away from the city and they were fighting a lot, I mean brutal fights and she liked to throw things so . . . there were only two beds in the lighthouse and inevitably my father would end up sleeping alone and I'd go and hold him in the middle of the night. Sometimes he was still crying, and I held him, because I was scared he'd do something stupid, and I held him, night after night and one day I woke up and he wasn't there anymore, he'd gone missing. They looked for him for days, my mum was in an absolute state, hating herself for shouting at him that last night, calling him pathetic, yeah, and then after about a week he washed ashore in Denmark. They sent an ambulance back to Sweden with his body.

Edward   Fucking hell, Ellie. I didn't know that's how it happened.

Ellida   Finn said something last night that shocked me. And I don't know why it shocked me because it was obvious.

Edward   What did he say?

Ellida   That you and him are the same age.

Edward   But that's not . . . I mean . . . there's a difference . . .

Ellida   Is there?

Edward   I don't know.

Ellida   I need to spend a bit of time not chasing my dad. Yep. I need to miss him for a while. I don't know if I'll come back.

Edward   Okay.

Ellida   And I know if I want to have a child that my body is well and truly not on my side but I can't rush this process just because of that, I tried that too many times already, and I know I might be throwing away my best chance at happiness and you'll probably fall in love with someone within a year and just when I'm ready to meet you again you'll tell me –

Edward   I won't.

Ellida   You probably will. And that'll just be my shit luck. But if you don't.

Edward   I won't.

Ellida Then it'll be the best reunion sex you've ever had. I promise that.

Edward I look forward to it.

Ellida Seriously do whatever you need to do. Don't hold on just for old times' sake, believe me, that's disastrous. Okay I'm going.

Edward I'll be here.

Ellida We'll see.

She goes.

Edward *takes it in. After a moment he gets in the pool. Lets himself fall under the water.*

An awfully long time passes.

Just when we think he's not coming back up, he does.

A huge yearning gasp.

The End.